TOOL MAKING FOR WOODWORKERS

TOOL MAKING
for
WOODWORKERS

Ray Larsen

photos by John Kelsey

CAMBIUM PRESS

Tool Making for Woodworkers
by Ray Larsen

ISBN 0-9643999-8-9

First printing: January 1997
Second printing: June 1998
Third printing: April 2002

Printed and bound in the United States of America

Published by
    Cambium Press
    PO Box 909
    Bethel, CT 06801
    203-778-2782
    www.cambiumbooks.com

TABLE OF CONTENTS

ACKNOWLEDGEMENTS

Good tools take my breath away and always have. Even as a small boy I spent a lot of time at my father's modest, cellar workbench trying to fathom their many mysteries. I've never been without a good set of tools, and when I got into blacksmithing some 25 years ago, it was only a matter of time before I gravitated to making tools exclusively. But I didn't get from there to here on my own. A lot of people helped me along the way, and to each and every one of them I am exceedingly grateful. I especially want to thank the late Chet Hood, Bill Masciarelli, Gerry Galuza, Fletcher Coddington, David Zatz, Fran Merritt, Jerry Wood, Howie Evans, Peter Ross, Melany Runyan, Bob Montgomery, Susan Barbieri Montgomery, Jack Riddle, Joe Hannigan, Jim McCollum, George Sturtevant, Tony Millham, John Hietala, David Draves, Charlie Merritt, Robert Larson, my mother, Irene Larsen, and my wife, Joan Norris.

Ray Larsen

CLASSES IN TOOL MAKING

If reading this book has piqued your interest in tool making, you'll be interested to learn that weekend tool making workshops are offered by Ray Larsen year-round at Genuine Forgery.

These workshops provide two intensive days of hands-on instruction, with participants mastering the basic elements of tool making through lectures, demonstrations, and, most importantly, by actually making some of the tools discussed in this book.

For a comprehensive workshop brochure or for further information, contact:

Genuine Forgery
1126 Broadway
Hanover, MA 02339
Ph: (617) 826-8931

EARTH, AIR, FIRE AND WATER

Earth, Air, Fire and Water: Blacksmithing is absolutely elemental. Dig iron and coal out of the earth. Prepare the hearth and light the coal, tend the fire and fill it with air to make it totally hot. Now heat the steel to near white-hot, then hammer on it. Work hard to forge the shape you need. Quench in cool water.

If you obey the ancient mysteries, if you pay attention to what you see and smell, if you hold your mouth just right, you can make tools. Real steel tools. Hammers and tongs, knives and axes, adzes and chisels, calipers and turning tools. With steel tools you can work wood, build a house, make a machine, fly to the moon.

The first time I met Ray Larsen, more than 20 years ago, he was itching to demystify the blacksmith's craft in the pages of *Fine Woodworking* magazine. Ray knew a way you could make a working forge out of an old barbecue. He could explain how to tell good steel from bad just by looking at sparks from the grinder. Would anybody be interested in such arcane stuff as this?

Well, sure. Ray's article about how to build a barbecue forge turned out to be a keeper. People asked for reprints (it's on page 29), and they sent in photos of improved forges they'd built for themselves. But whether or not you actually made a forge for yourself, Ray's information had the whiff of authenticity. It was the kind of lore people keep for their own. Because

you <u>could</u>, you see, in case civilization were to collapse. You could make a start at starting over. You could find an old barbecue and some kind of refractory cement, and there'd be a lot of scrap iron and steel lying about, and even if you couldn't dig coal, you could always make charcoal. You could pound out a pair of tongs and an axe and a chisel, and there you'd be, on the rebound, upward once again.

There's another way that blacksmithing is fundamental. Like woodworking, like making ceramic pots, hammering on hot iron and steel changes more than the workpiece. All the truly fundamental crafts are two-way transactions with the material world. Always there are two workpieces in play. One of them is obvious, it's the plank of wood or lump of clay or bar of iron or steel. The other is not so obvious, because it's you. The changes occur with exquisite slowness, but they are inexorable. Working with basic materials like clay and wood and iron and steel also works on the artisan. It changes the body and it refocuses the mind's eye.

Ray Larsen knows how that happens. If you've bought a hand-forged woodworking tool made at Genuine Forgery, you've sampled one side of the fundamental equation. Now try blacksmithing for yourself. Taste the power of making tools to suit your own hands. Feel how the hot steel works on your self.

—*John Kelsey, Publisher*

INTRODUCTION

Sooner or later, most woodworkers want to know more about the tools they're using: How they're made, what they're made of, and whether they can be made or modified to perfectly suit a specific task.

Many want to know if it's possible or practical to make their own tools.

It is both possible and practical. As with most things, tool making is composed of a finite number of basic elements. Master these elements, and you're on your way to becoming your own tool supplier.

Most woodworkers already have some of the equipment needed for tool making, including a grinder, bench honing equipment, and a heavy-duty drill press. But it does require investment to buy and set up the rest of the necessary equipment, and a substantial block of time to learn the necessary skills. You should ask yourself how serious your need is for special, high-quality tools before deciding to make the effort. Some devoted woodworkers quickly resent the time taken away from their first love to produce tools they really don't need.

Once you learn tool making, however, you need never again worry about tools breaking, or not holding an edge, or ruining your work. Less time struggling with tools means more time producing high-quality work. And the most exotic tools are readily available.

Need a special shape for turning the inside of a box? It's there for the making. Many woodworkers find that a tool especially designed for a job enables them to produce pieces others can't, or to produce them faster or more economically. The right tool for the job means superior work.

After your initial investment, you will also begin saving time and money. There's no more waiting until special tools are available, or running around searching them out, or shelling out the high cost of having them made by a specialist.

You'll also be able to repair and modify tools. A chipped screwdriver can be reshaped at a fraction of the cost of replacing it; an old parting tool can be reworked for a few cents to turn a special configuration.

In addition, you will have the capacity to forge special pulls, latches, hinges, and other one-of-a-kind hardware that can lend a unique finishing touch to your projects and products.

Ultimately, the success you see in tool making will be in direct proportion to the energy you put into it. But after studying and practicing the techniques and projects in this book, you will have learned everything you need to know, and practiced doing everything you need to do, to make woodworking tools on your own setup in your own shop. You'll know how to make tools "quick and dirty" for one-time use only. And you'll know how to make tools that perform perfectly and last well beyond your lifetime.

You will also transcend the planet in the process. Forging tools is an extraordinary experience, and once you have done it, you will be forever changed by it. You will clearly see, perhaps for the first time, how tools <u>really</u> do what they do and why. You will see completely new possibilities for the kinds of work you undertake in the future. You will see woodworking in a different light than ever before.

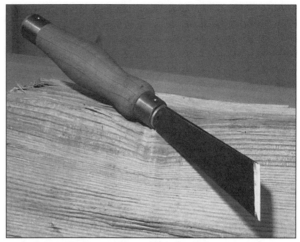

Learn how to make this skew chisel on page 110.

Make this hollowing adze starting on page 120.

Learn how to make this turner's hook on page 130.

Make this mortising chisel starting on page 136.

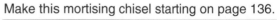

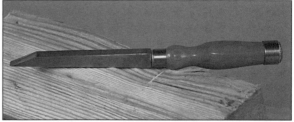

A lot of what you will learn in this book will be on the order of guerrilla tool making. This is not a text for purists; improvisation and innovation will be emphasized. For the woodworker, what works is what counts in tool making. In addition to learning how to make tools and set up shop, you'll gain access to the special world of blacksmithing. As a result, you will be able to lay your hands on any tool-making technology you require. And you'll learn a great deal about the many resources available to the tool maker.

One of the most important resources available is the Artist-Blacksmiths' Association of North America (ABANA), a nationwide organization of blacksmiths. Every woodworker contemplating making his or her own tools should join ABANA. It is a wellspring of knowledge and assistance on every aspect of blacksmithing, and its quarterly publication, the Anvil's Ring, contains hundreds of pieces of useful information in every issue, from tips on technique to the latest suppliers of quality tools and equipment.

ABANA will also put you in touch with the Association chapter in your area. These groups sponsor periodic meetings where members swap information, learn new skills, buy and sell equipment, and generally further the cause of blacksmithing. By getting involved on the local level, you'll meet dozens of like-minded craftsmen, and learn first-hand what's what in your neck of the woods.

See the appendix at the back of this book for information on joining ABANA.

DEMYSTIFYING TOOL MAKING

To most woodworkers, tool making is shrouded in mystery. But anyone
with modest hand skills can learn to make his or her own tools.
There are six basic elements to tool making:

1. Choosing the right steel. Steel producers throughout the world routinely manufacture several thousand different types of steel each year in a wide range of configurations, from sheet and plate, to bars, to complex shapes like I-beams and angle iron. What's suitable for making tools and what isn't? In Chapter 1, you'll learn exactly what kinds of steel to use, and where to buy them at reasonable prices.

2. Selecting a method of heating the steel to make it forgeable. What's the best way to get your steel "forging hot"? In Chapter 2, you'll learn a number of ways to do the job, including a tried-and-true method for building your own tool forge from scrap materials.

3. Obtaining the equipment needed to shape the steel while it's hot. How much equipment do you need to get started? Where can you buy it? And how much will it set you back? In Chapter 3, you'll find a wealth of information on purchasing new and used equipment, as well as tips on how to make rather than buy many of the items you'll need.

4. Becoming proficient in forging. Can you really teach yourself how to forge woodworking tools from a book? You can, by following the step-by-step projects detailed in words and photographs. The forging discussion is in Chapter 5. The tool projects begin with Chapter 8.

5. Learning the necessary finishing technology. How do you get from a rough-forged tool to one that's razor sharp and ready to go? In Chapter 6, you'll learn everything you need to know about finishing, including many "tricks of the trade".

6. Mastering the art of heat treating to develop the desired properties in the finished tool. Are annealing, hardening, and tempering as complicated as they sound? Can tools really be heat treated properly in the home workshop? In Chapter 7, you'll get all the information you need to produce high-quality woodworking tools that will take and hold a keen edge for years to come.

1 TOOL MAKING STEEL

Domestic and overseas producers make a wide range of steels suitable for woodworking tools.

These include high-carbon, water-hardening steels (so-named because they contain large amounts of carbon and are hardened by quenching them in water), a variety of tool steels, several alloy steels, and one type of stainless steel.

The tool steels include "W" (for water-hardening) type tool steels; "0" (for oil-hardening) type tool steels; "A" and "D" (for air-hardening) type tool steels; "H" (for high-speed) type tool steels, and "S" (for shock-resisting) type tool steels.

HIGH CARBON STEEL

High carbon, water-hardening steel is the steel most commonly used. It's being phased out by many large manufacturers these days because parts and products made of it are difficult to heat treat consistently in large quantities.

But that's got nothing to do with us. We're

making tools one at a time, and high carbon steel is one of the best steels available.

What exactly is high carbon steel?

All steel contains some carbon; it is the amount of carbon a steel contains that determines its hardenability and thus, its ability to do work. Only the high carbon steels, or steels containing more than 0.50% carbon, contain enough carbon to be of use in making woodworking tools.

Under the American Iron and Steel Institute (AISI) classification system, carbon steels carry the designation 10 followed by the decimal percentage of carbon they contain. Thus, high carbon steels range from AISI classification 1055 steel (containing 0.55% carbon), to AISI classification 1095 steel (containing 0.95% carbon).

In the AISI system, high carbon steel containing more than 1.00% carbon is classified as W-1, a full-fledged, water-hardening tool steel. W-1 can contain as much as 1.5% carbon, depending on the make.

Generally speaking, high carbon steel's hardenability — that is, its ability to take and hold an edge — increases with the amount of carbon it contains. But this happens at a price. As high carbon steel's hardenability increases, its toughness decreases. This is the fine line tool makers must walk when they work with high carbon steel: How to balance hardness and toughness to get just the right amount of each for the tool in question.

CARBON STEELS

SAE Number	AISI Number	Carbon C	Manganese Mn	Phosphorus P (Max.)	Sulphur S (Max.)
1006	C1006	0.08 max.	0.25-0.40	0.040	0.050
1008	C1008	0.10 max.	0.25-.50	0.040	0.050
1010	C1010	0.08-0.13	0.30-0.60	0.040	0.050
1015	C1015	0. 13-0.18	0.30-0.60	0.040	0.050
1016	C1016	0.13-0.18	0.60-0.90	0.040	0.050
1017	C1017	0.15-0.20	0.30-0.60	0.040	0.050
1018	C1018	0.15-0.20	0.60-0.90	0.040	0.050
1019	C1019	0.15-0.20	0.70-1.00	0.040	0.050
1020	C1020	0.18-0.23	0.30-0.60	0.040	0.050
1021	C1021	0.18-0.23	0.60-0.90	0.040	0.050
1022	C1022	0.18-0.23	0.70-1.00	0.040	0.050
1024	C1024	0.19-0.25	1.35-1.65	0.040	0.050
1025	C1025	0.22-0.28	0.30-0.60	0.040	0.050
1026	C1026	0.22-0.28	0.60-0.90	0.040	0.050
1027	C1027	0.22-0.29	1.20-1.50	0.040	0.050
1030	C1030	0.28-0.34	0.60-0.90	0.040	0.050
1033	C1033	0.30-0.36	0.70-1.00	0.040	0.050
1034	C1034	0.32-0.38	0.50-0.80	0.040	0.050
1035	C1035	0.32-0.38	0.60-0.90	0.040	0.050
1036	C1036	0.30-0.37	1.20-1.50	0.040	0.050
1038	C1038	0.35-0.42	0.60-0.90	0.040	0.050
1039	C1039	0.37-0.44	0.70-1.00	0.040	0.050
1040	C1040	0.37-0.44	0.60-0.90	0.040	0.050
1041	C1041	0.36-0.44	1.35-1.65	0.040	0.050
1042	C1042	0.40-0.47	0.60-0.90	0.040	0.050
1043	C1043	0.40-0.47	0.70-1.00	0.040	0.050
1045	C1045	0.43-0.50	0.60-0.90	0.040	0.050
1046	C1046	0.43-0.50	0.70-1.00	0.040	0.050
1049	C1049	0.46-0.53	0.60-0.90	0.040	0.050
1050	C1050	0.48-0.55	0.60-0.90	0.040	0.050
1052	C1052	0.47-0.55	1.20-1.50	0.040	0.050
1055	C1055	0.50-0.60	0.60-0.90	0.040	0.050
1060	C1060	0.55-0.65	0.60-0.90	0.040	0.050
1062	C1062	0.54-0.65	0.85-1.15	0.040	0.050
1064	C1064	0.60-0.70	0.50-0.80	0.040	0.050
1065	C1065	0.60-0.70	0.60-0.90	0.040	0.050
1066	C1066	0.60-0.71	0.85-1.15	0.040	0.050
1070	C1070	0.65-0.75	0.60-0.90	0.040	0.050
1074	C1074	0.70-0.80	0.50-0.80	0.040	0.050
1078	C1078	0.72-0.85	0.30-0.60	0.040	0.050
1080	C1080	0.75-0.88	0.60-0.90	0.040	0.050
1085	C1085	0.80-0.93	0.70-1.00	0.040	0.050
1086	C1086	0.82-0.95	0.30-0.50	0.040	0.050
1090	C1090	0.85-0.98	0.60-0.90	0.040	0.050
1095	C1095	0.90-1.03	0.30-0.50	0.040	0.050

APPLICATIONS FOR VARIOUS HIGH CARBON STEELS

Decent, general-purpose tools can be forged from AISI 1055 steel, but its use isn't recommended. It's a good steel for scrapers, but not much else, and the smith looking to forge high-quality woodworking tools needs to work the higher grades to get satisfactory results.

In days past, when high carbon steel was the only steel available for tool making, blacksmiths developed elaborate tables for using the various high carbon steels. Here's a brief summary of their thinking on woodworking tools, along with some of the applications we've worked out at Genuine Forgery:

AISI 1055/1060
Scrapers.

AISI 1060/1070
Augers.

AISI 1060/1078
Wedges, froes, sledges, wrecking and pry bars, screwdrivers.

AISI 1078/1080
Axes, adzes, hammers.

AISI 1080/W-1
Inshaves, drawknives, scorps, block knives, hollowing shaves, chisels, carving tools, plane irons, reamers, scratch awls, gouges, turning tools, routers, floats, spoke shave and travisher blades, knives, gravers, burnishers, drills, and shears.

SOURCES FOR HIGH CARBON STEEL

It's best to forge tools out of new steel whenever possible. New steel is preferable because the tool maker knows exactly what he's working with and can select exactly the right type for the job. No matter how good the smith is at identifying used steel, there is always an element of risk.

When buying new steel of any kind, be sure to obtain a copy of the manufacturer's data sheet covering the steel you purchased. This sheet gives the exact composition of your steel, along with important information on the right forging and heat treating temperatures.

Because the minimum amount of steel that can be bought directly from a steel maker is prohibitively large for the individual tool maker, woodworkers should first look to local service centers or steel warehouses to meet their high carbon steel needs. Some steel service centers are independently operated, others are sales branches of major steel producers. If in doubt, select a company that advertises itself as a member of the Steel Service Center Institute (SSCI), an organization of reputable steel suppliers.

Every major urban area in America also has its own eclectic assortment of "second tier" steel suppliers. These are generally small, independent operators located on the fringes of industrial neighborhoods. They're not as reliable as the SSCI guys, and they don't always know what they're talking about. But get out there and look them over as well. You might find something great for short money, and they're <u>always</u> interesting.

Many local and national industrial supply houses also carry some high carbon steel. Their selection is, for the most part, limited to short lengths of small round, square, and rectangular (flat) bars of W-1, but what they do sell is good stuff. Large suppliers to contact for this kind of steel include the MSC Industrial Supply Co. and Wholesale Tool Co. branches in your area, and the Travers Tool Co., Flushing, NY. See the appendix at the back of this book for information on contacting supply houses.

Local manufacturers who use large quantities of high carbon steel in the products they make are also possible sources. These companies are sometimes willing to sell small amounts of new stock to individual tool makers as a good will gesture. Remember to be polite. These guys are doing you a favor.

Still another place to try is your local scrap or

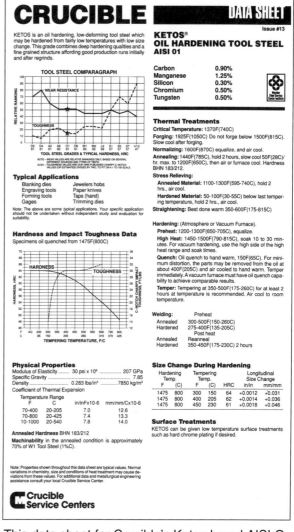

This data sheet for Crucible's Ketos brand AISI O-1 oil hardening tool steel shows the kinds of information contained in a data sheet.

salvage yard. These businesses sometimes buy useable stock from area manufacturers who no longer need a particular size or type. They also buy stock that got too bent, too nicked, too groaty, or too rusty for use in a factory but which is fine for forging. You can pick up good steel in these situations for very little money.

It's also a good idea to start attending industrial auctions in your area. Metalworking companies are liquidated on a regular basis, and some unused stock is almost always included in such sales.

If you do attend an auction, don't rely on the auctioneer or his staff for information about steel at the sale. They usually don't know much. Rather, search the auction crowd for guys who once worked at the plant. There are always some in attendance, and they <u>know</u> what's what.

If none of these sources of high carbon steel work for you, don't despair. Drop by the blacksmith, welding, and fabricating shops in your area. See if these guys have something, or can put you onto something. They're unfailingly nice people who will be glad to help as long as you're polite and treat them respectfully.

One thing to keep in mind is that tool making steels are usually produced and sold in bar form. These bars run 6 to 20 feet in length and come as rounds, squares, round-cornered squares, rectangles (known as flats in the trade), hexagons, octagons, and, occasionally, hollow rounds. They are never shaped like railroad rail, I-beams, channels, angles, or reinforcing bars (rebar).

Some high carbon and oil hardening steels are also produced in sheet and plate.

USED HIGH CARBON STEEL

Although new high carbon steel is best, used high carbon steel can also be recycled to make excellent tools.

Millions of tons of high carbon steel have been made into various parts and products over the years, and hundreds of thousands of those parts and products can be bought for next to nothing at junk yards, flea markets, and garage sales. They can also be had free of charge and in large quantities at most town dumps.

It's important to note that these parts and products have already been heat treated. Heat treating is the application and/or manipulation of heat to bring out desired properties in a piece of tool making steel.

Old woodworking chisels, for example, have been heat treated to a high degree of hardness so their bevels will take and hold a good edge. Springs, on the other hand, have been heat treated to exploit a piece of steel's potential for elasticity.

Heat treating is carefully explained later in this book. What you need to know here is that steel that has been previously heat treated must be carefully annealed or softened before it can be reforged into woodworking tools. But this is rarely a problem, and annealing is thoroughly covered in the heat treating section.

Here are some high carbon steel parts and products to look for, along with the type of high carbon steel they're probably made of:

Heavy-duty jackhammer bits. Heavy-duty points and chisels (with $1^{1}/8$ inch and $1^{1}/4$ inch hexagonal shanks above and below the collar), used in large jackhammers for pavement breaking: *AISI 1078. (see photo on page 24)*

Stoneworking tools. All chisels, drills, and facing-type hammers used for working stone: *AISI 1080/W-1.*

Some typical high carbon steel products that can be recycled into woodworking tools.

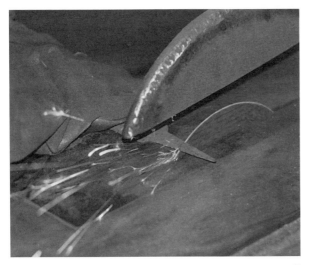

A regular tablesaw can drive an abrasive cutoff wheel, so you can use it to saw scrap metal to the size you need.

Heavy sledges for working stone: *AISI 1060/1080.*

Files and rasps: *AISI 1095/W-1.*

Mattocks, picks, and grub hoes: *AISI 1070/1078.*

Plow discs, plowshares, and harrow disks: *AISI 1080.*

Plow beams: *AISI 1070.*

Hay rake teeth: *AISI 1095.*

Mower blades: *AISI 1055/1085.*

Most coil springs. Including large car and truck springs, garage door springs, lawnmower starter springs, bed springs, and the like: *AISI 1085/1095.*

Old woodworking tools. See "Applications for Various High Carbon Steels" on page 13 for probable AISI composition.

Old car and truck leaf springs. (Make sure they're old; new leaf springs are liable to be made of a less desirable alloy steel): *AISI 1085/1095.*

Clutch discs: *AISI 1060/1085.*

Music wire: *AISI 1085.*

Power loom needles: *AISI 1085/1095.*

SAW BLADES

Many magazine articles have been written over the years about making woodworking tools out of old saws. Discarded saw blades turn up everywhere. Unfortunately, the steels they're made of are formulated for that application and that application only, and are not especially well suited to making woodworking tools in general.

WORKING WITH HIGH CARBON STEEL SCRAP

Working with high carbon steel scrap in the shop sometimes presents a real challenge. Big, old truck springs, for example, are heavy and unwieldy.

One way to deal with this is to saw your scrap into manageable pieces. Most woodworking supply houses carry abrasive saw blades that can be mounted in your circular or table saw. They're just the thing for cutting heat-treated, high carbon steel scrap down to size.

Coil springs can also pose a problem, but here's an easy way to uncoil them: Heat the spring clear through, then slip it over a short piece of round bar clamped in a vise. When you grip one end of the spring with a pair of tongs and pull, the spring will straighten quickly and easily.

TOOL STEEL

One of the major advances in the steel industry in the last 100 years has been the development of scores of "super steels" known as tool steels to meet the increasingly stringent demands of industry.

As cutting speeds of lathes increased, for example, steel makers had to come up with new formulations that would allow lathe tools to stay sharp at very high temperatures. The result was the development of high-speed type tool steels.

Many types of tool steel can be used to great advantage in making woodworking tools. But tool steels are not without drawbacks. For one thing, they're expensive; some cost more than six dollars a pound, even on the discount market. For another, they can be extremely difficult to work and heat treat in the small shop.

Nevertheless, a growing number of modern knife and tool makers are using these steels to make wonderful stuff, and most guerrilla tool makers will want to try their hand with them. Here are some of the tool steels we have found useful in making woodworking tools:

AISI W-2

Like the W-1 steel mentioned earlier, W-2 is a high carbon, water-hardening type tool steel. Its principal distinction from straight high carbon steel is the inclusion of vanadium in its make-up, which greatly increases its hardenability and toughness.

AISI W-4

Another high carbon, water-hardening tool steel, but containing .25% chromium. This addition gives it exceptional edge-holding ability, but makes it more difficult to hand forge.

AISI O-1

An all-purpose, oil-hardening tool steel suitable for everything from knife blades to dies. Will not hold quite as good an edge as the previously mentioned tool steels, but is easier to heat treat. A good choice for tools with complicated shapes.

AISI D-2

A high-carbon, high-chromium, air-hardening tool steel. Some cutlers consider it <u>the</u> steel for long, thin blades.

AISI A-2

A fine, all-purpose air-hardening tool steel with better-than-average toughness.

AISI M-2

An all-purpose, high-speed type tool steel used for tools (such as turning tools) that are subjected to high temperatures during use. Will not hold as good an edge as the water-hardening tool steels, but will not lose its temper. Difficult to forge.

AISI M-42

An exceptional, cobalt-type high-speed tool steel capable of extreme hardness. The Mercedes of high-speed tool steel.

AISI S-5

A silicon-manganese type shock-resisting tool steel. It combines good edge holding capability with phenomenal battering strength. Ideal for striking tools, but difficult to forge by hand.

TOOL STEELS

Class	C	Mn	Si or Ni	Cr	V	W	Mo	Co
WATER-HARDENING TOOL STEELS								
W1	0.60-1.40	-	-	-	-	-	-	-
W2	0.60-1.40	-	-	-	0.25	-	-	-
W3	0.60-1.40	-	-	-	0.50	-	-	-
W4	0.60-1.40	-	-	0.25	-	-	-	-
W5	0.60-1.40	-	-	0.50	-	-	-	-
W6	0.60-1.40	-	-	0.25	0.25	-	-	-
W7	0.60-1.40	-	-	0.50	0.20	-	-	-
SHOCK-RESISTING TOOL STEELS								
S1	0.50	-	-	1.50	-	2.50	-	-
S2	0.50	-	1.00Si	-	-	-	0.50	-
S3	0.50	-	-	0.75	-	1.00	-	-
S4	0.50	0.80	2.00Si	-	-	-	-	-
S5	0.50	0.80	2.00Si	-	-	-	0.40	-
OIL-HARDENING COLD-WORK TOOL STEELS								
O1	0.90	1.00	-	0.50	-	0.50	-	-
O2	0.90	1.60	-	-	-	-	-	-
O6	1.45	-	1.00Si	-	-	-	0.25	-
O7	1.20	-	-	0.75	-	1.75	0.25opt	-
AIR-HARDENING MEDIUM-ALLOY COLD-WORK TOOL STEELS								
A2	1.00	-	-	5.00	-	-	1.00	-
A4	1.00	2.00	-	1.00	-	-	1.00	-
A5	1.00	3.00	-	1.00	-	-	1.00	-
A6	0.70	2.00	-	1.00	-	-	1.00	-
A7	2.25	-	-	5.25	4.50	-	1.00	-
HIGH-CARBON HIGH-CHROMIUM COLD-WORK TOOL STEELS								
D1	1.00	-	-	12.00	-	-	1.00	-
D2	1.50	-	-	12.00	-	-	1.00	-
D3	2.25	-	-	12.00	-	-	-	-
D4	2.25	-	-	12.00	-	-	1.00	-
D5	1.50	-	-	12.00	-	-	1.00	3.00
D6	2.25	-	1.00Si	12.00	-	1.00	-	-
D7	2.35	-	-	12.00	4.00	-	1.00	-
CHROMIUM HOT-WORK TOOL STEELS								
H11	0.35	-	-	5.00	0.40	-	1.50	-
H12	0.35	-	-	5.00	0.40	1.50	1.50	-
H13	0.35	-	-	5.00	1.00	-	1.50	-
H14	0.40	-	-	5.00	-	5.00	-	-
H15	0.40	-	-	5.00	-	-	5.00	-
H16	0.55	-	-	7.00	-	7.00	-	-
TUNGSTEN HOT-WORK TOOL STEELS								
H20	0.35	-	-	2.00	-	9.00	-	-
H21	0.35	-	-	3.50	-	9.50	-	-
H22	0.35	-	-	2.00	-	11.00	-	-
H23	0.30	-	-	12.00	-	12.00	-	-
H24	0.45	-	-	3.00	-	15.00	-	-
H25	0.25	-	-	4.00	-	15.00	-	-
H26	0.50	-	-	4.00	1.00	18.00	-	-
MOLYBDENUM HOT-WORK TOOL STEELS								
H41	0.65	-	-	4.00	1.00	1.50	8.00	-
H42	0.60	-	-	4.00	2.00	6.00	5.00	-
H43	0.55	-	-	4.00	2.00	-	8.00	-
TUNGSTEN HIGH-SPEED TOOL STEELS								
T1	0.70	-	-	4.00	1.00	18.00	-	-
T2	0.85	-	-	4.00	2.00	18.00	-	-
T3	1.05	-	-	4.00	3.00	18.00	-	-
T4	0.75	-	-	4.00	1.00	18.00	-	5.00
T5	0.80	-	-	4.00	2.00	14.00	-	8.00
T7	0.75	-	-	4.00	2.00	14.00	-	-
T8	0.80	-	-	4.00	2.00	14.00	-	5.00
T15	1.50	-	-	4.00	5.00	12.00	-	5.00
MOLYBDENUM HIGH-SPEED TOOL STEELS								
M1	0.80	-	-	4.00	1.00	1.50	8.50	-
M2	0.85	-	-	4.00	2.00	6.25	5.00	-
M3	1.00	-	-	4.00	2.40	6.00	5.00	-
M4	1.30	-	-	4.00	4.00	5.50	4.50	-
M6	0.80	-	-	4.00	1.50	4.00	5.00	12.00
M7	1.00	-	-	4.00	2.00	1.75	8.75	-
M10	0.85	-	-	4.00	2.00	-	8.00	-
M15	1.50	-	-	4.00	5.00	6.50	3.50	5.00
M30	0.80	-	-	4.00	1.25	2.00	8.00	5.00
M33	0.90	-	-	3.75	1.15	1.75	9.50	8.25
M34	0.90	-	-	4.00	2.00	2.00	8.00	8.00
M35	0.80	-	-	4.00	2.00	6.00	5.00	5.00
M36	0.80	-	-	4.00	2.00	6.00	5.00	8.00
LOW-ALLOY SPECIAL-PURPOSE TOOL STEELS								
L1	1.00	-	-	1.25	-	-	-	-
L2	0.50-1.10	-	1.00	0.20	-	-	-	-
L3	1.00	-	-	1.50	0.20	-	-	-
L4	1.00	0.60	-	1.50	0.20	-	-	-
L5	1.00	1.00	-	1.00	-	-	0.25	-
L6	0.70	-	1.50Ni	0.75	-	-	0.25 opt	-
L7	1.00	0.35	-	1.40	-	-	0.40	-
CARBON-TUNGSTEN TOOL STEELS								
F1	1.00	-	-	-	-	1.25	-	-
F2	1.25	-	-	-	-	3.50	-	-
F3	1.25	-	-	0.75	-	3.50	-	-
LOW-CARBON MOLD STEELS								
P1	0.10 max	-	-	-	-	-	-	-
P2	0.07 max	-	0.50Ni	1.25	-	0.20	-	-
P3	0.10 max	-	1.25Ni	0.60	-	-	-	-
P4	0.07 max	-	-	5.00	-	-	-	-
P5	0.10 max	-	-	2.25	-	-	-	-
P6	0.10	-	-	3.50Ni	1.50	0.20	-	-
P20	0.30	-	-	-	0.75	-	0.25	-
PPT	0.20	1.20	4.00Ni	-	-	-	-	-
OTHER ALLOY TOOL STEELS								
6G	0.55	0.80	0.25Si	1.00	0.10	-	0.45	-
6F2	0.55	0.75	0.25Si 1.00Ni	1.00	0.10 opt	-	0.30	-
6F3	0.55	0.60	0.85Si 1.80Ni	1.00	0.10 opt	-	0.75	-
6F4	0.20	0.70	0.25Si 3.00Ni	-	-	-	3.35	-
6F5	0.55	1.00	1.00Si 2.70Ni	0.50	0.10	-	0.50	-
6F6	0.50	-	1.50Si	1.50	-	-	0.20	-
6F7	0.40	0.35	4.25Ni	1.50	-	-	0.75	-
6H1	0.55	-	-	4.00	0.85	-	0.45	-
6H2	0.55	0.40	1.10Si	5.00	1.00	-	1.50	-

SOURCES FOR TOOL STEEL

When it comes to buying tool steel, there's good news and bad: The good news is that it's readily available, the bad news is that it's expensive.

Every major urban area in America has service centers that stock tool steels in a wide range of sizes and shapes. There are also several large national discounters to buy from. One that we have had excellent results with over many years is ALBRACO Metals Corp., Carle Place, NY. They'll sell you any kind of tool steel you want (except water-hardening types), in any quantity, at reasonable prices. See the appendix for information on contacting ALBRACO.

What's reasonable?

Here's a sampling of prices from a recent (1996) ALBRACO circular:

AISI M-2 rounds, $3.75/lb.; AISI M-42 rounds, $5.10/lb.; AISI D-2 rounds, $2.25/lb.; AISI A-2 rounds, $1.82/lb., and AISI O-1 rounds, $1.42/lb. Prices will vary somewhat according to size and shape, and do not include cutting or shipping, which are extra. How much steel is one pound? A small axe or adze weighs between one and two pounds. A carving chisel weighs less than one pound.

Most local and national industrial supply houses also carry a variety of tool steels in many sizes and shapes. They only offer it in short lengths, but that's rarely a problem as tool making seldom requires long lengths of steel.

USED TOOL STEEL

If you decide to make tools from tool steel, start with new rather than used steel. Used tool steel can be difficult (and sometimes impossible) to anneal and work.

It can also be difficult to identify. Some scrap yards in major industrial areas specialize in recycling tool steels, so this is the first place to check. A few even guarantee the composition of what they sell, at additional cost. Most scrap yards, however, don't segregate their tool steel and can't really tell you what they do and don't have.

If you do buy some scrap tool steel and you're not sure what it is, try grinding a piece of it on a clean grinding wheel and observing the pattern of sparks that results. This is called the spark test. Many steels exhibit signature spark patterns when ground that reveal their composition. Some smiths keep samples of steel of known composition next to the grinder. These can be used as comparisons when spark testing steels of unknown composition. There are old timers in the trade who are astoundingly good at applying the spark test, but it's an acquired skill, so don't be discouraged when it takes you a while to get the hang of it.

ALLOY STEEL

Technically speaking, all steels are alloys. But in the current marketplace, the term alloy steel refers to a specific group of steels developed largely under the auspices of the Society of Automotive Engineers (SAE).

These steels were formulated to solve specific problems in industry at the lowest possible cost. With the exception of SAE/AISI 52100, they are inferior to both high carbon steel and tool steel for tool making, but they can be used in a pinch when nothing better is available.

Here are some useable alloy steels:

SAE/AISI 4140

This general purpose, oil-hardening alloy steel has been widely used in industry. In recent years, tool makers have used it for picks, mattocks, digging bars, cold chisels, and some pave-

High-carbon steel: Gold/white color, considerable bursting and sparking around the wheel.

Medium-carbon steel: Some bursting sparks, some sparking around periphery of wheel.

High-speed tool steel: Similar to high-carbon steel, but with fine explosions. Reddish streamers, no sparking around wheel.

Cast iron (not forgeable): Short, thin, brick-red streamers, very little sparking.

Low-carbon steel: Streamers from wheel are straight and light-yellow in color. Some sparking.

Wrought iron (inappropriate for blades): Similar to low-carbon steel, yellower streamers, practically no sparking.

Sparks from a grinding wheel can help identify steel. Keep known samples by your wheel for comparison.

Two typical pavement breaker tools. The two-inch chisel with a hexagonal shank above the collar is made of AISI 1078. This is an excellent steel for making axes, adzes, and hammers. The broad-bladed asphalt cutter with a round shank above the collar is made of SAE/AISI 4140. This steel is only marginally useful for making woodworking tools and should only be used when nothing better is available.

ment breaker tools. These are good sources for used 4140. Pavement breaker tools made of 4140 are generally those with round shanks above the collar such as clay spades, asphalt cutters, and wedges.

SAE/AISI 4063
A good, all-around alloy with enough carbon to hold a decent edge and still be plenty tough. Used for making marlin spikes, a good source for used stock.

SAE/AISI 9260
A silicon-manganese, oil-hardening alloy steel widely used in making tools for small electric demolition hammers. It only holds a fair edge, but is almost as tough as S-5 tool steel. These tools can be found at every flea market for little or no money.

SAE/AISI 52100
This high-carbon, chromium type steel is known in the industry as bearing steel because it's used extensively in the manufacture of bearing components. It's also used widely by custom knife makers. It's the best of the alloy steels for making woodworking tools because it has a lot of carbon in it (up to 1.1%, depending on maker), but is somewhat difficult to work because of its chromium content.

All of the other alloy steels are to be avoided. Be especially wary of the family of alloy steels known as "free machining" or "free cutting" steels. Some contain lead, which improves the material's machinability but causes it to emit toxic fumes when heated to forging temperatures.

STAINLESS STEEL

Until very recently, stainless steels had little if any application in the making of woodworking tools. Stainless steels provide exceptional rust and stain resistance, but even the most sophisticated types will not hold as good an edge as straight high carbon steel. Furthermore, they are difficult to work in the small shop.

It is true that stainless steels now predominate in the manufacture of commercial cutlery, but it is their rust-resisting — rather than their edge-holding — properties that have led commercial knife makers to abandon high carbon steel in favor of stainless steels. In fact, increasingly strict public health regulations required it, so if you want a kitchen knife that will really hold an edge, buy the next rusty, old, high-carbon "Dexter" brand you see at a flea market, or make your own out of 1095.

Or try a brand new stainless steel just developed by Carpenter Technology Corp. of Reading, PA.

The numbers for steel don't lie, and the numbers for Carpenter's new 440-XHTM are awesome. Here's what Industrial Heating, a leading trade publication, had to say about the stuff recently:

"The air-hardening, high-carbon, high-chromium, corrosion resistant steel designated 440-XHTM can attain a hardness of Rc 62 (the hardness of a typical Swiss carving chisel). In addition, the composition of this material has been balanced so that it can attain a minimum of Rc 60 when air cooled from a broad range or hardening temperatures (1850 to 2000 degrees F). Thus, it is more forgiving during heat treatment than similar steels.

"The design of this steel allows its consideration for those applications for type 440C stainless that require higher hardness, such as bearing assemblies (including balls and races), cutlery, needle valves, ball check valves, valve seats, pump parts, ball studs, bushings and wear resistant components. Because of its hardness, this steel also is a candidate for D-2 tool steel applications requiring more corrosion resistance, such as blanking dies, forming dies, extrusion dies, drawing dies, forming rolls, edging rolls, beading rolls, master tools, intricate punches and slitting cutters."

In short, now there is a stainless steel that tool makers can use to produce excellent tools, though it is expensive and hard to get.

POWDER METALLURGY

For many years, manufacturers have employed powder metal (P/M) technology in the mass production of complex parts. In P/M technology, a mold is machined to the exact size and shape of the desired part. The mold is then filled with metal in powder form and placed in a press, where the powder is consolidated. The resulting "green" part is then sintered in a furnace. When the sintering is done, the part is ready.

P/M molds are expensive to make, but the technology has proved cost effective when producing parts in high volume that would otherwise require a great deal of individual machining.

In recent years, steel producers have come to realize that P/M technology has other advantages as well. One major advantage is that steels produced in powder form are purer and more homogeneous than steels cast in ingots (the traditional method used to manufacture tool making steels). Tests have shown that tool making steels produced using P/M technology can outperform traditional steels — sometimes by as much as 50% — due to their superior purity.

This has led some steel producers, such as Colt's Crucible Specialty Metals Division in Syracuse, NY, to offer bars of tool making steels that have been produced using P/M technology.

Crucible's CPM REX M2S high speed steel is a typical steel made using P/M technology. Here's what the company has to say about it:

"CPM REX M2S High Carbon, produced by the Crucible Particle Metallurgy Process, is an improved quality product compared to conventionally produced material. This unique process results in homogenous macro and micro sections, exhibiting a finer carbide particle size and freedom from carbon segregation. CPM tools will have a finer grain size, better toughness, and superior grindability in the heat treated condition, as well as improved stability and distortion."

Tool making steels produced with P/M technology cost more and are harder to find than steels produced by conventional technology. But they offer substantial improvements in performance, and budding tool makers might want to try their hand with them.

2 HEATING THE STEEL

The steels used in tool making must be heated clear through to extremely high temperatures (1800°F to 2250°F, depending on type) before they can be forged.

Several recent articles in woodworking magazines have suggested heating the steel with an acetylene or propane torch. This is not recommended. These torches do not generate the type of heat needed, and using them usually proves frustrating and, ultimately, off-putting.

When heating tool making steel for forging, it's extremely important that the steel be heated clear through to the correct temperature. Hand-held torches can't do this, and steel that has been heated up this way tends to break up inside when it's forged. You can't see this kind of damage on the surface, but it will cause the tool to fail either during heat treatment or in service.

THE FORGE

The simplest way to heat steel properly for tool making is in a forge, in which a blast of air is applied to a coke, charcoal, or coal fire.

The infusion of oxygen supplied by the blower elevates the temperature of the forge fire to steel-working levels.

As with all great things, the beauty of the forge lies in its simplicity. In 1977, in an article in *Fine Woodworking* magazine, I described one easy method of building a small forge out of junk. Dozens of woodworkers have since told me their experiences in successfully building similar, and often, better, forges. For blowers (to generate the air blast), they used everything from vacuum cleaners (my suggestion), to hair dryers, to small, high-speed industrial fans enclosed in home-made housings of wood and sheet metal. For hearths, they used everything from discarded barbecue grills (my suggestion) to junked automobile brake drums.

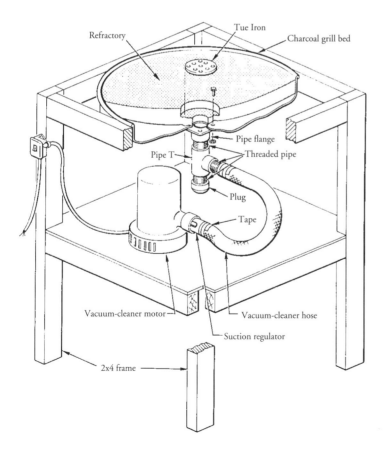

Refractory · Tue Iron · Charcoal grill bed · Pipe flange · Pipe T · Threaded pipe · Plug · Tape · Vacuum-cleaner motor · Vacuum-cleaner hose · Suction regulator · 2x4 frame

BUILDING YOUR OWN FORGE

A serviceable forge can be constructed from readily available materials. The bed is built from a new or used stamped-metal outdoor grill. A hooded type (not shown here) makes essential venting easier. Or a hood can be made from sheet metal and a stovepipe. The factory-made tubular legs are discarded in favor of a heavy-duty 2x4 frame with braced 2x4 legs. The bed should be at workbench height. The center hole in the bed is enlarged to accept a 2-inch pipe flange; a T-fitting introduces the air blast and a plug is loosely fitted beneath for ash clean-out. A vacuum-cleaner suction regulator or similar device regulates the blast. Refractory is troweled around a suitable form, such as a plastic bleach bottle with a 2-inch pipe inserted through its bottom, placed over the center hole. A tue iron cut from heavy-gauge sheet metal and drilled or punched is laid over the 2-inch blast opening in the bed.

If you decide to build your own forge, one key to success is lining the hearth with a suitable refractory or ceramic, heat-resisting material. Refractory comes in many forms, but for this application, use Kast-Set, a hydraulic type manufactured by A.P. Green Refractories Co., Mexico, MO. It comes as a powder, is mixed with water, and is troweled into place like cement. Look in the Yellow Pages under <u>Refractories</u> for a supplier in your area.

If you choose not to make your own forge, new forges are readily available from dealers specializing in blacksmithing equipment. One very reliable national supplier is Centaur Forge Ltd., Burlington, WI (see appendix). Their catalog contains not only forges but everything you could ever want in the way of equipment, though some of it is pricey.

Used forges of every imaginable size and shape are also easy to find. Try flea markets, garage sales, swap meets, scrap yards and used equipment dealers. Also check the classified advertising publications that circulate in your area. They often contain ads for used forges and equipment. You should be able to find a good, usable forge this way for around $100.

In many used forges, the fire pot or tuyere at the center of hearth will be burned out from years of heavy use and will have to be replaced. But this isn't a problem because Centaur and other dealers carry fire pots in many sizes and shapes, one of which can be adapted to the forge you buy.

Whatever type of forge you pick, equip it with an electric blower and place the on-off switch close by for easy access. Bellows and hand-cranked blowers work just fine, but can be hard for the beginning tool smith to manage along with everything else that's going on.

Fit your forge with an electric blower if at all possible. Bellows and hand-cranked blowers are more difficult to manage.

SETTING UP YOUR FORGE

Forging generates smoke and soot that must be vented out of the shop. So regardless of the type of forge you buy, you'll need to install a hood over its hearth. Some forges come with integral hoods. If yours doesn't, you'll need to make your own or have one made up at a local sheet metal shop.

I like a hood that is suspended from the shop ceiling rather than the type that bolts to the hearth. A suspended hood gives you complete access to the hearth from all sides. This helps you work large, awkward pieces.

Ideally, a forge should be vented with 12-inch heavy-duty, galvanized smokepipe running straight up through the roof. Sidewall venting, even when it incorporates an induced draft mechanism, is only marginally acceptable and should be used only as a last resort. Remember that your smokepipe will get hot when the forge is in use. Make sure it's located safely. Be equally careful of how you handle hot ashes; they can burn your shop down if disposed of improperly. So can hot steel if you put it down in the wrong place. Also make sure that your forge is not located near any flammable materials. It's not uncommon for sparks to fly into the shop while you're managing your fire.

Forging also produces quite a bit of scale and dirt, so take as much time as you need to figure out where a forge fits best in your particular setup. Every shop is unique. Your forge should be conveniently available, yet far enough away for safety. A room or shed next to the wood-working shop is often ideal.

Whatever location you pick, make sure your forge is situated in a dimly lighted, or semi-dark, space. It's very important to see the different colors steel exhibits when heated to various working temperatures. Harsh light or direct sunlight can wash the color out of steel, making it impossible to judge its color correctly.

A suspended hood gives good access to your fire. Note that the blower switch is mounted at right on the hood, within easy reach.

· SAFETY TIP ·

Keep an industrial type fire extinguisher handy just in case a problem develops. There are local companies in most areas that specialize in supplying and servicing these units. Check the Yellow Pages under Fire Extinguishers for the name of a company near you.

FUEL

Forges can utilize coke, charcoal, or coal for fuel, and each has its good and bad points:

Coke. Coke is an industrial, coal-based fuel that is very easy to work in the forge. It yields a good, deep, lasting heat. It doesn't produce a lot of clinker, or impurities, to clog up the forge, and it is the easiest of the three fuels to manage.

But coke is expensive and generates a lot of irritating dust. It can also be hard to find outside major urban areas. Often, when it can be found, it comes in large chunks that need to be crushed into finer pieces before they can be used. And whomping large, unwieldy lumps of coke with a heavy sledge is hard, dirty work.

Charcoal. Charcoal, made by the controlled burning of hardwood, was the earliest fuel used in forges. It is still employed in places like Old Sturbridge Village, the living history museum in Sturbridge, MA, for authenticity's sake (it was cheaper in the old days to buy locally-produced charcoal than to haul coal in from the coast).

Charcoal (the loose, lump type, not the briquettes, which contain useless binders) produces an excellent heat, but it can be hard to find in quantity. It also burns rapidly, and thus, requires considerable management.

Coal. Blacksmithing coal, a soft, low-sulfur type coal especially suited to forge work, is the fuel most widely used by blacksmiths today. It's readily available at reasonable cost, gives a deep, high heat, and is relatively free of impurities. Call the coal yards in your area for the name of the dealer who handles this product locally. Pick it up yourself, it's cheaper. Blacksmithing coal is also available from national suppliers like Centaur, but you'll pay a lot for shipping.

FORGE TOOLS

Regardless of the fuel you choose, a few, simple tools are required to manage the forge fire. These include a small, heavy shovel for adding fuel, a poker or two for adjusting the fire and lifting out clinker, and a long-handled watering can for shaping and controlling the fire. These tools are traditionally made by the smith.

BUILDING A COAL FIRE

Technically speaking, you don't burn coal in a forge, you use the forge to convert the coal to coke, which becomes the fuel you are using. This requires fire management skills that take practice to develop fully. The beginning tool maker can teach himself enough in a week about coal fire management to make good tools, but it takes ten years to master the art.

To use your forge, you first need to make a small quantity of coke. To do this, wad three sheets of newspaper into a tight ball and set it afire with a match. When the ball is burning rapidly, place it in the forge's fire pot and cover it with several handfuls of fine kindling.

When the kindling is enveloped in flame, loosely pack six or seven handfuls of coal around the outside of the blaze. This will help contain and concentrate the fire.

Now slowly add a handful of coal directly to the fire. It will smoke heavily as it begins to burn. Start your blower and apply a light blast to increase the fire's intensity.

Continue adding small amounts of coal and air to your fire until you have an intense heat, then cut the blower back slightly. Wet down the coal on the perimeter periodically to keep the fire from dissipating. Continue to add fuel and adjust the blower as needed for about 30 minutes. Then cut the blower, pack the fire down tightly with the back of your forge shovel, and let it cool completely. This will take several hours.

When the fire is cold, break it apart with your shovel. You'll find that the coal has been reduced to two products: irregularly shaped lumps of coke, the high-grade carbon fuel you're looking for, and small bits of clinker, an amalgam of hard, glassy impurities driven out of the coal by the fire.

Clean out the fire pot, retaining the coke and discarding the clinker.

Now your forge is ready to use. When lighting it from now on, always start your fire with leftover coke rather than kindling. The following two pages illustrate how to do this.

The fire started with converted coke will catch a lot faster and burn a lot hotter and cleaner. Never again add fresh or green coal directly to the fire. Always add it to the perimeter of the blaze, where it can be converted to coke. Add this coke to the fire as more fuel is needed.

BUILDING A FORGE FIRE

1. To fire up your forge, crumple three or four full-sized sheets of newspaper into a tight ball.

2. Set the balled newspaper afire and place it in the center of the firepot.

3. Cover the burning newspaper with coke. Immediately introduce a moderate blast from the blower. This will help elevate the temperature of the fire and ignite the coke.

4. When the fire has caught, begin adding green coal to the outside of the fire. This will help concentrate the fire and ready the coal for coking up. Increase the blast to assure that the coke is burning well.

5. Pack the green coal around the coke fire, wetting it down slightly if needed. Keep a strong blast on the fire until you see a good, white heat at the center. Then cut the blast back somewhat to conserve fuel and keep the fire from burning out of control. The fire is now ready for forging.

BANKING THE FIRE

A coal fire will not continue to burn for long without periodic application of a blast, so when you want to bank your fire, stick the end of a hardwood bolt into the heart of the blaze and pack coke around it. This will keep the fire going for several hours.

The reason for this is simple: the combustion point of coal is so high that it needs an outside supply of oxygen to burn well. With the blast shut off, the temperature in the forge eventually falls below coal's combustion point and the fire dies. Adding a hardwood bolt with a much lower combustion point keeps a hot fire going in the center of the idle forge, and this tends to keep the coke burning longer.

When you're finished forging, cut the blast and pull the fuel away from the fire pot, storing it along the edges. This will cause the fire to die quickly, conserving fuel.

BUILDING COKE AND CHARCOAL FIRES

The same techniques used for building coal fires are used for building fires of commercial coke or charcoal, except that the initial coking step isn't necessary.

MANAGING THE FORGE FIRE

Whether the fuel is coke, charcoal, or coal, managing the forge fire is a complex, subtle art that can only be learned by doing.

Here are some things to keep in mind as you develop your fire management skills:

Keep your forge and fuel clean. Even the cleanest fuels contain impurities that are driven out in the form of clinker. This must be removed periodically from the fire or it will clog the fire pot. This, in turn, will reduce or cut the blast, spoiling the fire.

Clinker can be fished out of the fire pot with a poker while the forge is lit. To remove clinker, turn off the blower and allow the clinker to settle and collect at the bottom of the fire. This takes a minute or two. Then hook or lance it with your poker and carefully lift it away. This takes practice, but eventually, you'll be able to keep the forge running smoothly by periodically clearing away your clinker as it develops.

It's also important to clean out the fire pot and hearth every few days. Sift the contents through a screen to get rid of unwanted dust and small bits of clinker that eluded your poker. When coal heat was popular in the 30s and 40s, neat, ash-can-sized sifters were available at every hardware store for this purpose. They can still be found in junk shops. Sift your ashes into an ashcan and keep them on hand; they'll come in handy for performing certain heat treating operations.

Manage your blower. Always turn the blower off when you remove heated steel from the fire. This will conserve fuel and prevent the fire from racing out of control while you're working at the anvil.

Keep your fire properly aerated. Forge fires tend to collapse on themselves. This can reduce the effectiveness of the blast and inhibit proper combustion. Use your poker or shovel periodically to keep the fire loose and burning freely.

There is an optimal density for a forge fire, but it has to be experienced. Experiment until you can consistently get a fire that works well for you.

Keep your coal wetted down. The coal on the perimeter of your forge fire will begin to burn out of control after the forge has been running

Some typical pieces of clinker.

awhile. Keep the fire from spreading by wetting down the coal as needed. This will also help concentrate the fire and assist the ongoing coking process.

Manage your blast. It will take practice to learn just how much air your fire needs. Too little air results in a starved fire that burns poorly. Excessive air results in an oxidizing fire which generates excessive scale or oxidation on the surface of your steel.

Tailor your fire to the job at hand. When you've learned your way around the forge a bit, you'll come to see that it's possible to build different types of fires for different jobs. Some jobs, for example, require a big, deep, long fire. Some, like heat treating small tools, require a small, loose fire. Experiment. Try different things. Teach yourself by doing.

THE FORGING FURNACE

Until very recently, small, one-man shops relied exclusively on the traditional forge for heat, while factories used forging furnaces capable of much higher rates of production.

The line between the two has blurred of late. Many modern blacksmiths have come to recognize the numerous advantages furnaces offer and have installed them in their shops with excellent results.

A forging furnace isn't radically different from a forge; it's basically a forge with a refractory-lined, metal box sitting on top of it. In fact, the earliest forging furnaces used coke or coal for fuel, and a few companies, like Mayhew Metal Products, Inc., the Shelburne Falls, MA, tool-making concern, still use coal-fired furnaces in some of their operations.

The refractory-lined enclosure, known as the firebox, serves to concentrate and homogenize the forging furnace's heat over a much larger area than a forge. It also helps the furnace develop a more penetrating heat that permits much more radical deformation of the workpiece.

The forging furnaces of today run on No. 2 fuel oil, propane, or natural gas, and are far more efficient than their coal-burning forebears. Some even incorporate electronic igniters that make them easier to fire up. One of the biggest advantages of furnaces, and one that every novice will appreciate, is that they require very little management once they're started.

There are two basic kinds of forging furnaces: Industrial, and Craftsman.

INDUSTRIAL FORGING FURNACES

Many of the forging furnaces designed and built for factory use will work equally well in your shop. Most of these furnaces are too expensive for the starting tool maker to purchase new; the cheapest furnace of this type runs around $3,000.

Not to worry. There are hundreds of forging furnaces on the used-equipment market, and they usually sell for a fraction of their original cost, even when they're in like-new condition.

Auctions of metalworking companies are a good source for used industrial forging furnaces, as are used equipment dealers. I've bought and sold more than a dozen used industrial forging furnaces over the years, and I've never paid more than $100 for one.

There are also several large national dealers who specialize in used industrial furnaces. Their prices are quite a bit higher, but most will provide some kind of guarantee.

A typical industrial-type forging furnace. Note the blower switch and the gas valve located on the gas pipe at the right.

Industrial forging furnaces come in two types:

COMMERCIALLY BUILT FURNACES
Several dozen companies in the country manufacture industrial forging furnaces. A lot of these furnaces are too big for the small shop, but some are not. One manufacturer to look for is the Johnson Gas Appliance Co. of Cedar Rapids, IA. Johnson makes a whole line of small, gas-fired forging furnaces that work well in the one-man shop, and replacement parts for their furnaces are available at reasonable cost.

SHOP-BUILT FURNACES
Many forging companies have traditionally built their own furnaces based on the knowledge and experience they have gained over years of working hot steel. Many of these furnaces were designed specifically for tool work, and are excellent candidates for your shop. Although these units are shop built, they employ standard components so finding replacement parts isn't usually a problem.

BUYING A USED FORGING FURNACE
So what should you look for when buying a used forging furnace?

The first thing you need to determine is whether the furnace was designed for forging or can safely generate the amount of heat required for forging, as is the case with many heat treating furnaces. There are literally hundreds of kinds of industrial furnaces on the market, and not all of them are suited to forge work. Many industrial furnaces top out at 400°F to 2000°F. Check the manufacturer's nameplate. If the furnace wasn't built to sustain a minimum of 2350°F, on up to a maximum of 3000°F, don't buy it. If there is no manufacturer's nameplate, talk to someone who used the furnace and can tell you what's what.

Once you've determined that a furnace will meet your temperature needs, check its overall condition. You don't need a lot of expertise here, just common sense. Here are some things to look for:

- Is the firebox's metal exterior burned through in places? Don't buy it.
- Is the refractory lining sound? A few cracks are okay, but if there are big chunks missing, pass on it.
- Are there cracks or holes in the exterior or interior burner hardware? Don't touch it.
- Are any parts loose or falling off? Forget it.
- Does the blower run smoothly? If it rattles and clanks, know that you're going to have to replace the bearings before you run it.

One thing to keep in mind is that forging furnaces usually look worse than they are. They all get pretty grungy, so examine them carefully. Don't dismiss a basically sound furnace because of cosmetics. I once gave away a furnace because I didn't want to bother relining it. The guy I gave it to is still running it just the way I gave it to him. He says it runs great.

By the same token, err on the side of safety. If you ain't sure, don't buy it.

Ideally, you should run a furnace before you buy it. But this is rarely possible.

CRAFTSMAN-TYPE FORGING FURNACES

The last ten years have seen the development of a whole new family of forging furnaces specifically designed for use by craftsmen. These small, table-top units are a major reason more and more blacksmiths are turning to furnaces.

To my mind, these furnaces are not as good as industrial furnaces. They don't get as hot, they don't generate as penetrating a heat, and they're a lot less durable. But they're safe, efficient, and readily available. And they're reasonably priced: You can buy one complete and

A typical craftsman-type forging furnace. Reasonably priced units like this are readily available and are excellent sources of heat for beginning tool makers.

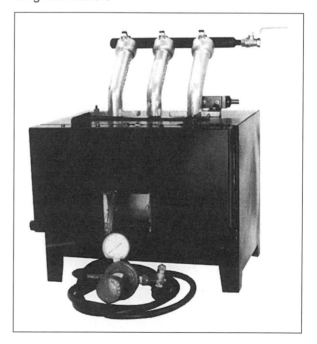

ready to run for under $500.

As with industrial forging furnaces, many of these craftsman-type furnaces employ electric blowers. But some utilize a venturi design that requires no blower and thus, no electrical hook-up. This can simplify location and set up.

Craftsman-type forging furnaces are available from Centaur Forge and other craft supply houses throughout the country. Mankel, which also makes industrial furnaces, Valley Forge & Tool, and NC Tool Co. are makers to look for.

BUILDING YOUR OWN FORGING FURNACE

In 1989, Robb Gunter, Karl Schuler, and Ronald Ward designed and built a small, high-efficiency gas forging furnace for use at Sandia National Laboratories in Albuquerque, NM. This furnace has proved so well suited for use in the small shop that the makers have drawn up a complete set of plans and materials list for it. They can be purchased through ABANA.

The furnace is a venturi type that requires no blower. It also employs a simple but effective recuperation system to preheat the air entering the furnace. This increases the furnace's efficiency while lowering its operating cost. In 1989, Gunter, Schuler, and Ward estimated the cost of the components for the furnace at around $175.

Building a Sandia-type forging furnace isn't for everyone. It requires considerable skill in sheet metal work, machining, and welding. But if you have some of these skills and think you might want to try your hand at it, contact Ray Rossi, president of the Rocky Mountain Smiths, an ABANA chapter based in Colorado. This group periodically holds workshops in which groups of interested smiths gather to build batches of Sandia furnaces.

Gunter, Schuler, and Ward weren't the first people to build their own forging furnace. Blacksmiths have been doing it for many years now, using off-the-shelf industrial components. But before you take something like this on, ask yourself if you have the time and skill needed to do the job. It's not something to dabble with.

INSTALLING YOUR FORGING FURNACE

Even the best-insulated furnace radiates a tremendous amount of heat, so safety is a major consideration in location. Be especially careful of what's directly above the site you pick. If you're working out of an old barn with low ceilings, hooding and venting are imperative or you'll only get to use your new furnace once.

As with a forge, make sure your furnace is situated in a semi-dark space that allows for good judgment of color.

Also make sure that your furnace sits on a solid base. I like a concrete pad with the furnace bolted to it. Have the wiring done professionally if you have any doubts. If your furnace uses a blower, make sure it is driven by an explosion-proof motor.

If the furnace you buy isn't equipped with a solenoid safety valve, have one installed before you run it. This valve will automatically cut the supply of gas to the furnace in the event of a power outage.

Take your own well-being into account as well. Make sure the area you pick is well ventilated for both safety and comfort. I once worked in a factory where the temperature in the forge shop routinely hit 130°F in summer, and that can take a lot of the fun out of tool making.

Furnaces produce a tremendous amount of heat. Be sure to use a hood for adequate ventilation.

FUEL

If you do decide to go with a furnace in your setup, pick one that burns propane or natural gas. Furnaces that run on No. 2 fuel oil are excellent; they're the most widely used type in the forging industry today. But they generate so much smoke and odor during heat-up and cool-down that they're not acceptable in most neighborhoods.

Of the two remaining fuels, natural gas is overwhelmingly superior. It generates just about the same amount of heat as propane, gives a much smoother range of heats, and costs about half as much as propane to operate. If natural gas isn't available in your area, propane is still an excellent, if more costly, alternative.

FURNACE POKER

If you decide to set up a furnace, keep a 4-foot poker made of ⅝-inch stock nearby. It can be used to fish awkward pieces out of the back of the furnace that you may not be able to reach with your tongs.

GAS SAFETY

If you choose to install a gas forging furnace in your shop, remember that leaking gas can be deadly. Have the gas fitting done professionally if you have any doubts whatever about your ability to do the job correctly. Some municipalities <u>require</u> that it be done by a certified professional.

If you ever smell gas in your shop, <u>do not</u> light your furnace, <u>do not</u> light a cigarette, and <u>do not</u> activate any electrical switch until the source of the leak has been found and corrected. When searching for a leak, always use soapy water or a commercial liquid, such as Western Enterprises Leak-Test, specifically designed for this task. <u>Never</u> use a lighted match.

Equip your furnace with a Maxitrol gas regulator. All furnaces require a regulator on the gas supply line to deliver the precise amount of gas required. Some furnaces come with a regulator. If yours doesn't, check the nameplate for the recommended pressure. Use Maxitrol-type regulators, manufactured by the Maxitrol Co., Southfield, MI. Because they're vented, if the regulator's diaphragm ever ruptures, the escaping gas is piped out of the shop. Maxitrol regulators are available from W.W. Grainger, Inc., and other industrial suppliers.

Finally, be sure to use high-temperature valve grease in your control valve. High-temperature grease is specially formulated to operate at elevated temperatures. Standard formulas can break down, causing the valve to leak.

SHUTTING DOWN

When you're finished forging for the day, it's a good idea to cool your furnace down slowly over a 10- or 15-minute period before turning it off. This will reduce thermal shock to the furnace's lining and significantly extend its life.

3 FORGING EQUIPMENT

When tool making steels are heated correctly to the right temperature, they become plastic and can be forged into virtually any shape by hammering them on an anvil. This is the blacksmith's art.

THE ANVIL

The central piece of equipment in this enterprise is the anvil. It is the single most important piece of forging equipment you will buy, so consider it carefully.

Anvils come in hundreds of styles, but the London pattern predominates because it is superior. It is the classic layout with a long, tapering horn and cutting table at one end and a shallow, square heel, containing hardie and pritchel holes, at the other. It has a rectangular face hardened all over. This combination of shapes allows the clever tool maker to generate many of the shapes he wants freehand. The photo at left shows my favorite anvil, a 486-pound London pattern Hay-Budden.

Double-horn anvils, which are widely used in Europe, are also suitable, but the shallow heel of the London pattern lets you forge pieces with tight bends that won't clear an anvil horn. Other specialty anvils, such as the hornless saw-maker's anvil, can also be used if nothing better is available.

The hardie hole is used for holding hardies and other square-shanked anvil tools. Their use will be discussed later. The pritchel hole is used for punching small holes. The cutting table is used to cut hot steel on and is not hardened.

As for size, bigger is better. Look for something that weighs at least 150 pounds. Anything smaller won't stand up to the tough steels used in tool making.

It's not easy to judge the weight of an anvil by looking at it.

English anvil makers, such as Peter Wright, sometimes stamped the actual weight of each anvil on one side. Examine an English anvil carefully and you may find three numbers. The first number represents hundredweights (112 pounds), the second represents quarter hundredweights (28 pounds), and the third represents pounds. Thus, an English anvil marked 215 weighs 257 pounds (224 + 28 + 5).

American anvil makers, such as Hay-Budden, sometimes stamped the actual weight in pounds on the sides of their anvils.

Most anvils, however, have no weight marking. The best way to judge the size of these anvils is to take several key measurements from them and compare these figures to the table below. The table is taken from a 1905 Hay-Budden catalogue. It specifically describes London pattern anvils manufactured by Hay-Budden, but can be used as a general guide for estimating the size of any anvil.

Approximate Dimensions of General Blacksmiths' Anvils According to a 1905 Hay-Budden Catalogue				
Weight in Pounds	**Face Inches**	**Horn Inches**	**Hardie Hole Inches**	**Pritchel Hole Inches**
80	$3^1/2$ x 12	$8^1/2$	$3/4$	$7/16$
100	$3^5/8$ x $13^1/2$	9	$3/4$	$7/16$
125	$3^3/4$ x 15	10	$7/8$	$9/16$
150	4 x $16^1/2$	$10^1/2$	$7/8$	$9/16$
175	$4^1/4$ x 17	11	1	$9/16$
200	$4^1/2$ x 18	$11^1/2$	$1^1/8$	$11/16$
250	$4^3/4$ x 20	$12^1/2$	$1^1/8$	$11/16$
300	5 x 21	13	$1^1/4$	$11/16$
350	$5^1/2$ x 22	$13^1/2$	$1^1/4$	$11/16$
400	6 x 23	$14^1/2$	$1^3/8$	$11/16$
450	$6^1/2$ x 24	$15^1/2$	$1^3/8$	$11/16$
500	$6^3/4$ x 25	16	$1^1/2$	$13/16$

BUYING AN ANVIL

New anvils are still easy to buy but they're expensive. A 165-pound Peddinghaus, for example, currently retails for $835.

So start by buying a good, used anvil. They're also pretty easy to find. Yard sales, flea markets, used equipment dealers, antique shops, and scrap yards are all places to look. Prices vary, but you should be able to buy a good, solid anvil for around $1 a pound.

The single most important thing to look for in a used anvil is a sound, flat face free of cracks, cuts, or gouges. The tools you forge will only be as good as the face of your anvil. Use a steel straightedge to spot valleys. A few hollows are okay, they can be used for straightening, but the face should be basically flat.

In recent years, it has become possible to repair almost any anvil face problem by corrective welding. This practice has become fairly widespread of late, but you should avoid anvils with faces that have been repair welded if at all possible. They are <u>never</u> as good as they were originally.

Another thing to look for in an anvil is a face with good, sharp edges. Edges tend to chip over the years. A few edge chips in a used anvil are inevitable, but extensive chipping signals an anvil that needs retiring.

Good anvils are made in several different ways. Here are four high quality types, in descending order of excellence:

ANVILS WITH FORGE-WELDED FACES

The best anvils are made by forge welding a high carbon steel face to a wrought iron body. This process produces a hard, extremely tough, resilient anvil capable of a great deal of work over a long period of time.

The best anvils of this type were made by Hay-Budden of Brooklyn, NY, and Peter Wright of England. Trenton and Arm and

Hammer anvils are also acceptable.

When considering anvils of this type, look at them from the side first. You should be able to see a regular line running the length of the anvil where the face was forge welded to the body.

Check the thickness of the face plate. An inch or more is good; anything under 5/8-inch won't hold up.

Also, look for evidence, such as chipping out, that the face is separating from the body. This sometimes happens to anvils with forge-welded faces, and anvils with this problem should be avoided.

One way to test the soundness of an anvil with a forge-welded face is to strike it moderately on the face with a 3-pound or 4-pound hammer. A clear ring and crisp rebound are signs of a sound, well-made anvil. Avoid limp clunkers.

The face of this 450-pound Trenton anvil has completely broken away in one corner.

FORGED STEEL ANVILS

Two German companies, Reflinghaus and Peddinghaus, currently produce anvils by forging them from a single block of high-grade steel. These are also excellent, but rarely turn up on the used market.

CAST STEEL ANVILS

Since the turn of the century, a number of companies have offered good anvils cast in one piece of high grade steel. Sodofors and Kohlswa, both of Sweden, are names to look for.

Recently, several American companies have also begun offering cast steel anvils. They are without exception inferior to their European counterparts, but are offered at attractive prices.

With cast steel anvils, older is better. Castings take years to cure, and the more they cure, the stronger they get. As with an anvil with a forge-welded face, a sound, cast steel anvil will give a good, clear ring when struck with a hammer.

Although good cast steel anvils are plenty tough, they aren't as tough as wrought anvils, and can be broken if misused. Avoid heavy sledge work on the horns and heels of these anvils and keep them warm in winter. They get considerably more brittle when it's cold out.

CAST IRON ANVILS WITH
HIGH CARBON STEEL FACES
In 1843, Mark Fisher of Fisher and Norris in Trenton, NJ, patented a method of making anvils that involves casting a specially formulated iron body onto a high carbon face and horn. These anvils produce a dull clunk when struck, but they're good anvils.

Face separation can be a problem with these anvils, so study them from the side carefully. If there's evidence of separation, don't buy. There are plenty of used Fisher and Norris anvils around but prices are sometimes artificially high. That's because they have an eagle motif cast into their side, which makes them sought after by tool collectors and antique buffs.

CAST IRON ANVILS

A number of industrial suppliers these days offer cast iron anvils for very little money. Avoid them, they are far too brittle for tool work. If you're not confident of your ability to spot cast iron, use an old cast iron window weight for comparison. The sides and bottom of a cast iron anvil will have a grainy surface similar to that of the old window weight. It will also clunk when struck with a hammer.

SETTING UP THE ANVIL

When in use, your anvil should sit hard by, and perpendicular to, your forge or furnace. A quick quarter turn has you forging your heated tool blank. Heated steel begins to cool the moment it's

Time is of the essence: Set your anvil hard by your forge so you can turn to face both with ease.

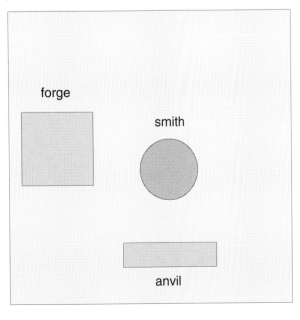

removed from the fire, so time is of the essence.

Traditionally, the anvil was mounted atop a knotty, white oak stump buried several feet deep in the shop floor. Knotty oak was used because the knots checked any splitting that developed from heavy use.

A permanent arrangement like this may not suit your situation. Mount your anvil instead on a hardwood stump that sits on the shop floor. This way it can be rolled out of the way when not in use.

The height of the anvil is critical. The face should sit level with the knuckles of your hammer hand as it hangs naturally at your side. This is a rule of thumb; the actual height may vary slightly. Your back will tell you exactly the right height for you.

Some blacksmiths suggest tipping the anvil face slightly away from you to help shed scale, the iron oxide flakes that develop on steel's surface when it's heated in an oxygenated fire. This is nonsense. Mount the face perfectly level. This gives a superior, predictable blow. It also provides the frame of reference for the shapes you are developing.

Traditionally, right-handed smiths set their anvil with the horn on the left; left-handed smiths with the horn on the right. It's been proven over time that the entire surface of the anvil can be worked more efficiently this way.

To mount your anvil, place 3 or 4 asphalt roof shingles on the top of your stump, set your anvil on top of them, and pin it to the stump with long spikes. The shingles help even out the rough, irregular bottom found on most anvils, which can cause the anvil to wobble dangerously when struck. They also lend just the right amount of give to each hammer blow. This actually enhances the blow. It also reduces shock and stress on the smith's elbow.

Ashley Iles, the noted English tool maker, reports that English smiths traditionally bed their anvil bases in horse manure to get the amount of "give" they desire.

If a hardwood stump isn't available, build up a heavy block out of pieces of hardwood clamped together with steel bands. Nail and glue the pieces together with construction adhesive to make the block as solid as possible

The post vise has a leg set in the floor so it can stand heavy pounding. This post vise holds a fuller ready for use.

THE BLACKSMITH'S VISE

Tool making requires a blacksmith's vise, also known as a post or leg vise. This is a special, rugged vise with a heavy, iron leg which is set in the floor of the shop for rigidity. You can hammer work in this type vise, and do serious twisting and bending in it. You can also clamp shaping tools in the blacksmith's vise and forge on them that way.

Don't buy a new vise; they're too expensive. Pay $50 to $60 for a good, used one with 5-inch or 6-inch jaws. They're still easy to find.

One of the things to look for in a blacksmith's vise is the condition of the jaws. They should be solid, and without cracks or chipping. They should be perfectly square to each other, and meet tightly and evenly when closed.

The vise's screw and box are also important. They should be free of chipping and excessive wear. If there's a lot of slop in the screw when you crank up a vise, don't buy it.

Don't worry if the spring, mounting bracket, or screw handle are missing. You can easily forge replacements.

MOUNTING YOUR VISE

To provide the necessary rigidity, the blacksmith's vise must be mounted firmly to a heavy bench or post buried in the ground. The leg should be set into the floor or a concrete pad poured especially for it. Blacksmiths have devised a variety of portable stands for their vises over the years, but they don't work well and usually take up more space than they're worth.

The vise is traditionally positioned so that the

tops of the jaws are level with the smith's elbow.

TONGS

Steel is a relatively poor conductor of heat, so it's possible to hold one end of a long bar in your hand while heating and forging the other end of it. This isn't possible with short workpieces, which quickly become too hot to handle. These workpieces must be held with tongs while they're being worked.

Tongs look and work like pliers, but have much longer handles to keep your gripping hand well away from the heat and to give increased leverage.

Tongs must hold the workpiece securely to do their job and thus, come in an infinite variety of shapes and sizes.

You can never have too many pairs of tongs, so I recommend you buy every reasonably priced pair that crosses your path. They're still easy to find at garage sales, flea markets, junk yards, antique shops, and industrial auctions. Reasonable to me is $5 a pair.

Look for tongs that are good and beefy. The jaws should match up well. A little play in them doesn't matter, you can tighten them with a couple of hammer blows. The exact shape of the jaws of the tongs isn't all that important either. They are quickly reforged to fit a particular job.

If you don't want to go to the trouble or expense of buying tongs, you can make your own. The same techniques used to make woodworking tools can be used to make forging tongs.

Vise-Grip pliers can be used in place of tongs to grip many size and shape workpieces. Keep a large pair near the forge for just that purpose.

A sampling of tongs showing the wide variety of sizes and shapes commonly used in the tool shop.

Tong rings lock the tongs onto the workpiece.

Purists deplore this practice, which makes it even better.

USING TONGS

Forge a few small, oval rings of different sizes out of 1/4-inch or so round stock and keep them by your tongs. These are quickly slipped over the tong's reins or handles, locking the tongs securely onto the workpiece. This eliminates the need to grip the tongs tightly at all times. It also allows you to concentrate on manipulating the workpiece on the anvil.

Cool your tongs periodically in the slack tub.

Cool your tools and quench your workpieces in a tub of slack, or soft, water. Half a whiskey barrel makes an excellent slack tub.

THE SLACK TUB

You'll need to keep a large tub of water on hand to periodically cool your tools in. Anything that will hold at least 20 gallons of water will do, but nothing beats half a whiskey barrel. You can find these at nurseries and garden centers. Buy at the end of the growing season and you can get one for around $20.

After a few years use, the steel bands on whiskey barrels usually rust through and fail. To repair, wrap a piece of chain around the barrel in place of the band and secure the ends of the chain with a long bolt. Taking up on the bolt tightens the chain, keeping the barrel watertight.

Slack tubs can freeze in winter. Stick a 3-foot piece of 2x4 in it when cold weather hits. It will prevent bursting.

The slack tub is also used for quenching tools during heat treatment. It is therefore important to fill it with soft or slack water only. A rain barrel can provide you with all you need.

Quenching tools in hard water is asking for trouble. The minerals present in hard water

cause the heated tool to cool unevenly, and cracking often results.

TOOLS

Quite a few special tools are used in forging. Fortunately, it's possible to buy virtually any kind of blacksmithing tool you might need. These can be bought new from suppliers like Centaur, or used at garage sales and the like. Often, second-hand dealers don't even know that a particular chunk of steel in a box in the corner is a blacksmithing tool. If you get out

A classic forging setup. The anvil, center fore-ground, is just a quarter step away from the forge, at left. Also readily available for quick action are a leg vise, at right, a swage block, rear left, and a large cone, rear right. Note the three handy quench tubs at right. They contain, from rear to front: slack water, brine, and slack water with a thin layer of light oil on top. A fourth tank containing commercial grade quenching oil is just out of view at far right.

Some useful hammers, including, from left: An 8-lb. sledge, a 4-lb. square-faced forging hammer, a 4-lb. bevel-faced hammer used to draw tapers, a 2-lb. square-faced forging hammer, and a 20-oz. cross peen hammer good for finishing work.

Some useful sledges, including, from left: A 4-lb. ball-peen type sledge, a 6-lb. sledge, and an 8-lb. sledge.

A flatter, at left, which is hammered along work-pieces to smooth and true their surfaces, and a set hammer, which is hammered into workpieces to produce clean, crisp 90-degree angles.

and really look, you can find a lot of good stuff for 50 cents to $5 a tool.

As with tongs, the woodworker with a tool making setup can also make his or her own blacksmithing tools.

Here are some of the tools you'll need:

Hammers. Many types and sizes of hammers are used in forging, but you only need two to start.

Your first hammer should be a 2-pound to 3-pound engineer's hammer. A hammer this size is heavy enough to do some damage without being too tiring to use. This is the hammer with which you will do 90 percent of your work. Sears engineering hammers work just fine.

Your second hammer should be something lighter, such as a small ball peen hammer. This will allow you to do lighter, finishing work.

Eventually, you'll want to make your own forging hammers. These should have square, slightly crowned faces and straight peens with flat faces. Make a 4-pounder for general use, and a 2-pounder for finish work.

Sledges. You'll also need two sledges for the heavy stuff, like punching eyes. The first should be the biggest sledge you can swing with one hand. Six pounds is good; eight is better. Cut the handle down to around 18 inches so you don't hurt yourself.

You should also keep a 10-pound or 12-pound sledge on hand for very heavy work. Don't try to forge with this by yourself; use it when a helper or striker is available.

Flatters and Set Hammers. These are heavy, handled tools with flat faces used to smooth forged surfaces. They are held over the heated workpiece and struck with a hammer.

Flatters should have slightly rounded edges

so they glide along the surface of the workpiece without digging in. Set hammers should have good, sharp, square edges as they are used to "set" or square up angles and offsets.

Hardies. A hardie is an upside-down chisel with a square shank that fits your anvil's hardie hole. It is used for cutting steel. In practice, the steel is held over the hardie and struck repeatedly with a hammer until the cut is made.

Hardies come in hot and cold types. Hot hardies have relatively thin blades that can slice through hot steel quickly. Cold hardies are much beefier to stand up to the battering of cold cutting.

It is important that your hardie fit snugly— but not too snugly—in your hardie hole. A loose hardie can bounce around in use, damaging smith and workpiece. A tight hardie can become wedged in the hardie hole, making it difficult to remove. This is true for all tools that mount in the hardie hole.

Beginning tool makers should <u>always</u> remove the hardie when not in use. It's easy to forget it's there. A nasty gash may result.

Hot Cuts and Hot Chisels. These heavy-duty chisels are used for cutting and incising hot steel on the anvil's cutting table or in the blacksmith's vise. Hot cuts are handled, hot chisels aren't.

Basic hot cuts and hot chisels have thin blades and straight cutting edges. The edges should bow slightly from front to back. This allows you to walk the cut or chisel along a line to facilitate long cuts. They can also have curved or specially shaped profiles for making special cuts.

Make sure your hot chisels are at least 12 inches long. Hot steel radiates a lot of heat, and holding a short chisel over a hot bar is sure to cause a bad burn. This rule applies to all hand-held blacksmithing tools.

A typical shop-made hardie, the hardie's square shank fits into the anvil's hardie hole.

Three hot cuts. Note the curved blade on the hot cut on the right which makes it easier to "walk" the tool down a long cut.

A cold cut, at left, and two cold chisels. As you can see, the blades of these tools are much beefier than the blades of hot cuts and hot chisels.

Some useful punches, including, from left: A small eye punch, a square punch, and three round punches of various diameters.

Cold Cuts and Cold Chisels. These tools are similar to hot cuts and hot chisels but are much beefier to stand up to the battering they take when cutting steel cold. The cuts are handled, the chisels aren't.

When making or buying hot or cold chisels, be sure they have square, hexagonal, or octagonal shanks. Chisels with round shanks always roll just out of reach when they're needed.

Hot and Cold Punches. These can be handled or not and are used to generate holes in hot and cold steel. Eye punches are shaped like a tool eye and are used hot to punch eyes.

Small square or rectangular punches with tapering points are known as pritchels. They are traditionally used to punch nail holes in horseshoes over the anvil's pritchel hole, but have uses in tool making as well.

Punches can also be made in virtually any shape to make decorative impressions.

Some typical eye drifts, including, from left: A large, hand-held, round-eyed drift for making adze eyes, and four hand-held or tong-held, oval-eyed drifts for making various size eyes with hour-glass cross sections.

Drifts. These are specially-shaped tools that are used hot to drift out or shape a previously punched or drilled hole to a desired profile. Drifts are frequently used to generate or dress eyes. Some drifts are handled, some not.

Three fullers used for spreading or setting off sections of work. The wider types, at left and at right, can also be used in conjunction with swages to generate curves and sweeps.

Fullers. These cylindrically-faced tools are hammered into heated workpieces to mark off areas for subsequent operations or to neck down. They are also used for drawing out.

Fullers come in two types. The ones with handles are called top fullers. The ones with square shanks designed to fit your hardie hole are called bottom fullers. They are used singly or in combination.

Fullers come in many lengths and widths to provide the variety of shapes smiths need.

Swages or Swedges. The opposite of fullers, these tools contain depressions for forging steel into special shapes. As with fullers, they come as top and bottom tools and can be used singly or in concert.

In their simplest form, swages contain a half-round groove to generate a cylinder form of a particular size, such as a tenon. They may also contain intricate impressions which are imparted to the steel when it is struck in them.

Spring Tools. In early times, smiths had a helper. This extra pair of hands allowed them, among other things, to position a workpiece between a set of fullers or swages while the helper banged away.

As time passed, smiths could no longer afford helpers and had to devise ways of doing complex forging with one pair of hands.

One development was linking top and bottom fullers and swages with a spring, which kept the top tool centered over the bottom tool. This eliminated the need for an extra hand to hold the top tool in place.

Spring tools aren't available new and rarely turn up used. They're something you'll have to make as the need arises.

On the left are top swages, on the right are the bottoms. Note the square shank on the bottom swages for fitting in the hardie hole.

Some typical spring tools. Note that the set on the left has a post on the bottom tool that fits in the anvil hardie hole. This leaves both of the smith's hands free.

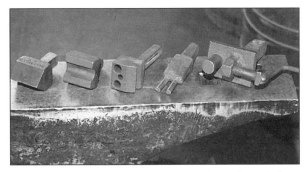

An assortment of anvil tools including, from left: a spreading tool, a typical swage, a sharpening swage used to sharpen tools, and two bending tools.

Here, a bick is used in the anvil's hardie hole to form a ring smaller than the anvil's horn.

ANVIL TOOLS

Hardies, bottom fullers, and bottom swages are known as anvil tools because they are designed to sit in the hardie hole. But they are not the only kinds of anvil tools. There are hundreds of different types. Some can be used in a variety of ways, others are designed for one specific step in a forging sequence.

Here are a few the tool maker will find useful:

Bicks or Bickerns. These are small anvil-shaped tools mounted on a heavy leg tenoned to fit the hardie hole. They are used to do work too fine for the anvil.

Cones or Mandrels. These are small, cone-shaped tools for forging rings and such that are smaller than the anvil horn.

Saddles. These tools straddle the anvil face and provide a flat forging surface thinner than the heel of the anvil. They are used, among other things, to forge the jaws of open-end wrenches too small to clear the heel.

Bending Forks. These are two-pronged tools. The workpiece is placed between the prongs and bent to the desired shape.

Cutting Plates. When cutting steel too big to fit on the anvil's cutting table, a cutting plate of mild steel is set down first to prevent the cut or chisel from scoring the anvil face.

CONES AND SWAGE BLOCKS

Cast iron floor cones up to 4 feet high and weighing well over 100 pounds are available new or used. They're not essential to tool making, but can be useful for forging tools with curved blades such as inshaves.

Large, cast iron swage blocks containing dozens of useful impressions are also available new or used. As with large cones, they're not essential, but they're very handy.

GUERRILLA TOOLS

It's nice to have a comprehensive set of traditional blacksmithing tools, but it isn't essential to making good woodworking tools. Improvised tools made from scrap can often accomplish a given task just as well.

Short pieces of heavy-walled pipe, for example, can be bolted to the anvil through the hardie or pritchel hole and used to generate various radiuses. Similar pieces of pipe cut in half and bolted to the anvil — open half up — make decent swages.

Don't become obsessed with acquiring tools. Use your head instead to figure out expedient alternatives. Devising innovative solutions to problems is one of the more exciting aspects of tool making.

A typical swage block weighing approximately 125 pounds. Note the variety of curves or sweeps that can be forged with this one tool.

Two pieces of guerrilla tooling. The heavy-walled pipe on the left is bolted to the anvil through the hardie hole and is used to form round shapes. The spring swages on the right were forged from a piece of 1/2-inch round scrap and are used for various kinds of fullering work. See the spring swages in use in the mortising chisel project on page 137.

4 SHOP SAFETY

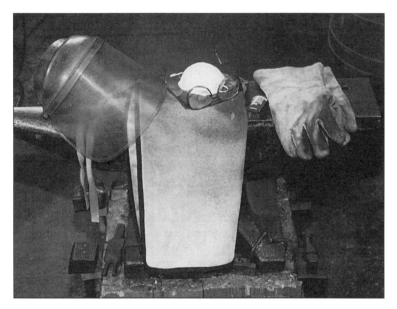

Before you light your first fire or take your first swing with a forging hammer, you need to give serious consideration to shop safety. Tool making is an inherently safe thing to do, as long as you follow a few simple rules and <u>never break them.</u>

The <u>never break them</u> part needs emphasizing. In my experience, accidents usually happen when you're tired or in a hurry and decide to cut corners. Don't take shortcuts where safety is concerned. Get into the habit of doing things by the book, every time out.

Here are some important safety considerations:

Eye Protection. It is <u>absolutely imperative</u> that you wear industrial-grade safety glasses whenever you are engaged in tool making. Your eyes are the most vulnerable part of your body. One steel splinter in the center of an eye will eventually destroy the sight in that eye.

Make a habit of putting your safety glasses on when you enter the shop. Keep them on until you leave. Do not perform <u>any</u> operation without them.

Don't stint in this area. If you have any question as to what constitutes a satisfactory pair of safety glasses, consult an eye doctor. And choose a style with side shields; they provide better protection.

Clothing. Hot, hostile stuff sometimes flies around during tool making. Always wear a heavy, long-sleeved shirt like a work shirt. It will prevent cuts and burns. Wear heavy jeans or work pants for the same reason.

Heavy, leather work boots are also essential for good protection and sure footing.

Gloves. Always keep a pair of heavy, leather welder's gloves on hand. Wear them whenever you are doing grinding or finishing work.

Never wear a glove on your hammer hand, it can cause the hammer to slip. Always wear a glove on your tong hand, it's vulnerable.

Gloves can wear out quickly in tool making. Have spares on hand. Replace a glove whenever its integrity has been compromised. I have sustained some serious cuts and burns over the years trying to get a little more mileage out of a worn $5 glove.

Grinding Protection. Tool making requires a considerable amount of grinding, and grinding requires even more protection. Always wear a heavy, leather apron when grinding. It will protect you from flying tools that get away from you, and will prevent your clothes from catching fire.

In addition, always wear an industrial-grade face shield or pair of protective goggles over your safety glasses. This will help assure that nothing gets to your eyes.

Hearing Protection. Tool making is a noisy undertaking, so hearing protection is advised. Industrial-grade ear muffs are the easiest and most comfortable solution. Choose a type approved by the Occupational Safety and Health Administration (OSHA) with a noise reduction rating (NRR) of 25 decibels or better.

Grinding protection should include safety glasses, a full face shield, a dust mask, a full-length leather apron, heavy leather gloves with long cuffs, and a long-sleeved work shirt. Do not stint in this area.

The ends of these two drifts have mushroomed from repeated, heavy use. If this mushroomed material isn't ground off periodically it can break off and fly around dangerously when the tool is hammered. The small bits of mushroomed steel on the anvil did, in fact, break off from the heavy drift in the photo. They were recovered to give you an idea of the amount of danger these projectiles pose.

Lung Protection. Finishing and grinding generate harmful particulates. Always wear a dust mask when performing these operations. If you're not satisfied with the performance of dust masks, look into respirators; there are many kinds available.

Hot Steel. Steel heated in a forge or furnace can inflict serious burns. Always handle hot steel with extreme caution. And remember, even when forged steel has no color, it can still be plenty hot. Black steel in the forging area should always be presumed hot until carefully proven otherwise. To test a piece of steel, move your hand toward it cautiously, sensing for heat. If you can get within an inch of it without sensing heat, tap it quickly with your fingertip. This will tell you how much heat, if any, remains in the piece.

Tool Safety. The striking surfaces of tools like hot cuts and fullers will mushroom from use. Grind or otherwise trim these tools periodically, or chunks of this material may fly off when struck, causing injury.

Never strike a hardened steel surface with a hardened steel surface. Dangerous, flying steel slivers are likely to result.

Drugs. <u>Never</u> use alcohol or other drugs when engaged in tool making operations. Make your tool making setup a drug-free zone, without exception.

Mental Attitude. The single most important element to shop safety is mental attitude. Always focus completely on the job at hand. Maintain your concentration. If your mind wanders, walk away from the job until you can get yourself under control again.

Some years ago, a friend of mine who was a grinder in a tool factory turned away from his machine while it was running to ask the foreman if it was time for lunch. When he turned back to his machine, he no longer had a left thumb. Tool making requires discipline.

It's also important to remember to <u>slow down</u> when a job starts to go bad. Everyone has a tendency to push harder when something goes wrong. This only makes things worse. Cool analysis, not bull-headedness, is what's needed. Excessive force does not solve problems; it makes trouble and often causes injury.

First Aid. Accidents happen to even the most careful craftsmen, that's why they're called accidents. When a mishap occurs, it's important not to panic. Examine the injury with as much clinical detachment as possible. If you even <u>think</u> your injury requires professional attention, get yourself to an emergency medical facility as quickly as possible. Early treatment can make a real difference.

And keep a well-stocked first aid kit on hand. This will enable you to deal effectively with those minor cuts, burns, and bruises that inevitably occur in even the safest of shops.

Every shop should have a good, comprehensive first aid kit close at hand. Its contents should include a cold pack, an eyewash solution, a variety of bandages, iodine or iodine wipes, burn ointment, an ace bandage, adhesive tape, and a topical analgesic.

5 FORGING TECHNIQUES

Now that you have the necessary equipment, and know how to use it safely, it's time to take a close look at the basic techniques tool makers use to turn raw stock into finished products.

TAKING A HEAT

Before you can start forging, you have to heat your steel clear through to a temperature that is (1) appropriate to the steel you are using, and (2) appropriate to the operation you intend to perform. This is called taking a heat.

Different steels are worked at different temperatures. Consult your data sheet or experiment to find the right temperature for the particular piece of steel you're working.

Different forging techniques also call for different temperatures.

But how do you know when your steel has been heated to the right temperature?

Steel takes on various incandescent colors as it is heated, and over the years, smiths have developed a good sense for judging the temperature of heated steel by the color it exhibits.

The chart at the bottom of the page provides <u>general guidelines</u> to help you generate the various temperatures needed in tool making.

Keep in mind when using this chart that judgment of color is to some degree subjective and that colors change in different lights.

Also keep in mind that it takes considerable practice to accurately judge the temperature of all the various tool making steels under all conditions. Don't be discouraged if you burn up a few pieces of steel while you're learning.

One tip is to keep a close eye on the scale your fire is generating on the surface of your steel. The scale should form in light, gray flakes. When the scale starts forming in large, black sheets, you're about to burn up your steel. You'll know you burned your steel when it starts giving off bright, white, bursting sparks and crumbles under the hammer.

When taking a heat, be sure to heat your steel slowly and uniformly so that the heat penetrates clear through it. This is called soaking and is especially important when taking a first heat.

You can sometimes tell if you've achieved a penetrating heat by studying the end of the workpiece being heated. When shadowy, black spots appear on the end's surface, it's ready to forge.

This doesn't always happen, however, so err on the side of caution here. A 1-inch square piece of tool-making steel should soak for 30 seconds or so before it's removed from the fire for its first forging. A soaking time of 20 seconds is satisfactory for subsequent forgings.

Smaller pieces require correspondingly less soaking time.

As noted earlier, if you forge steel that is cold at the center, it will develop interior occlusions or flaws that will cause the tool to crack or break later on.

Color	Temperature	Application
Faint Red	930° F	Lowest visible temperature; not suitable for forging.
Blood Red	1075° F	Finishing and packing.
Dark Cherry	1175° F	Finishing, lowest possible for drawing.
Medium Cherry	1275° F	Drawing.
Cherry	1375° F	Drawing, some bending.
Bright Cherry	1450° F	Drawing, bending.
Salmon	1550° F	Drawing, bending.
Dark Orange	1680° F	Drawing, bending, some cutting.
Orange	1725° F	Drawing, cutting, bending.
Lemon	1830° F	Drawing, cutting, bending, punching.
Light Yellow	1975° F	Drawing, upsetting.
White	2200° F	Some drawing, upsetting. Highest possible temperature for most tool making steels before they burn.

THE FIVE BASIC TECHNIQUES

If you were to watch forging by a great smith like Peter Ross, the master blacksmith at Colonial Williamsburg, your first impression would be of a wild blur of incomprehensible action. But if you sat and studied him awhile, you would begin to see that he was actually performing a few basic operations over and over again.

Forging steel is really simple; there are only a few things you can do to it. In fact, there are only five basic forging techniques used in tool making. They include drawing, cutting, bending, punching, and, occasionally, upsetting.

DRAWING

Drawing, also called pulling or hammering out, is the technique most frequently used in forging. Drawing is defined technically as *reducing the cross section of a bar of steel while lengthening it,* and in that definition lies the key to forging most tools.

To make a tool, basically, you start with a bar or piece of steel whose cross section is equal to the largest cross section of the tool you want to make. You then systematically hammer the bar into the various cross sections or shapes you need, reducing the cross section of the bar and lengthening it as you go.

If you want to make a copy of a tool, fill a large jar with water and mark the water line. Immerse the tool you want to copy and mark the new water line. The volume of water displaced by the tool is the volume of steel needed to make the tool.

Remove the tool and slowly insert a bar of steel into the jar. When the water rises to the tool's displacement level, you know how much of that bar will be needed to make that tool.

Yet another way to determine what size steel to start with is to make a model of the desired tool out of Plasticine or modeling clay. Plasticine works a lot like steel. If it takes a four inch piece of one inch round Plasticine to make your tool, that's about the amount of steel it'll take to forge one.

Drawing requires controlled hammerwork that takes time to master. When the hammer face strikes the workpiece, the force of the blow tends to spread the steel in all directions. This is fine if you are trying to spread the steel, as when making a wide blade. But if you want the steel to move in one direction only, as when pulling the tang of a drawknife, you will have to strike counter blows to channel this spreading in the desired direction.

Fullers are often used to aid in the drawing process. Fullers driven in perpendicular to a bar tend to lengthen the bar only, reducing the need for counter blows, or squaring up. Fullers can also be used to spread a bar by hammering in a series of impressions in line with the bar. This will spread the bar without lengthening it significantly.

Fullers can also be used to set off areas for drawing and to generate certain shapes. You can also do light fullering work with the cross peen of your hammer.

What is a typical drawing sequence?

To begin drawing a tool, carefully heat the bar to as high a heat as it can stand without burning. Get the piece really hot. The most common mistake beginning tool smiths make is failing to get the workpiece hot enough. Remember this old tool shop adage: If you're not burning up a few blanks each day, you're not forging hot enough.

When your steel reaches the correct temperature for drawing, which is a light yellow for high carbon steel but somewhat lower for most tool steels, quickly remove it from the fire and start hammering. Steel starts to cool the second it leaves the fire, and as it cools, it changes

Using a hand-held fuller to spread or draw a workpiece. Note that the hammer is raised well above the smith's head to deliver maximum power.

Drawing out the tang of a skew chisel.

color. When the steel cools to a cherry red, stop hammering and return it to the fire. Drawing it further at this point can damage it.

Really good smiths hold their heated steel just off the face of the anvil between hammer blows. That's because the anvil acts, among other things, as a heat sink, sucking heat from the steel whenever it comes in contact with it.

When drawing down, keep in mind that thin sections require less heat than thick sections. As you draw down, manage your fire so that you don't overheat your steel.

Drawing requires more feel and more blacksmithing sense than any other operation; it is as much art as mechanical manipulation. It is easily learned, but takes practice to learn well.

Start out in your shop by drawing a few, simple, predetermined shapes, such as wedges and long, square, tapered points. This will give you a feel for how hot steel moves. It will also show you what you can and can't do. If you want to forge a round section, for example, you'll find that it's best to forge it down square first, then round it up at the end.

The most important thing at the outset is to

develop a comfortable rhythm with the hammer. Use your entire arm to strike each blow. Swing from the shoulder, not the elbow or wrist. A few heats will give you a feel for how the hammer tends to cock itself for the next blow. Go with this feeling until you're comfortable with it.

Pace yourself. Start with slow, light blows. When you feel you're in control, pick up speed and increase velocity to generate more power.

Set your feet firmly, shoulder length apart. Raise your hammer above your head and strike each blow in the center of the anvil. One of the biggest problems beginning forgers encounter is holding the workpiece square and true on the anvil. When your tong hand dips, turns, or wanders, your hammer blows won't produce the shape you're looking for. The workpiece must be presented correctly on the anvil at all times if the work is to proceed as desired.

In the beginning, you will find yourself choking up on the hammer handle, both to improve control and to conserve energy. But the best blows are struck when the hammer is

When drawing out, stand close to the anvil and swing from the shoulder. This will help you produce good, accurate, heavy blows without putting undue strain on your wrist and elbow.

A good, balanced stance is essential if you are to generate strong, accurate blows.

gripped at the end. The handle, after all, is a lever, and more leverage is better. In forging, there is no substitute for power.

With each heat, your steel will develop surface oxide or scale that flakes off as it is forged. If you want your tool to have a smooth finish, keep a wire brush at the anvil and vigorously brush the scale off the steel before hammering it. Forging scaled steel tends to pit its surface.

When a particular length of steel has been drawn by hand, it will exhibit a rough, uneven surface. This surface can be smoothed out, if desired, by hammering it with a flatter. Flatters can help generate very smooth surfaces and good, even planes. Do this and other finishing work at the lower forging temperatures.

When striking a tool like a flatter, always keep your eye on the flatter's striking surface rather than on the workpiece. This will enable you to strike a good, clean blow, and reduce the chance of missing the tool and hitting something vulnerable, like your hand. Pause every few blows to check your progress.

Tool makers draw a lot of tapered cross sections or bevels, and bevels require special handling. Forging a bevel lengthens the thin portion of the bar it's being made from more than the thick portion. This, in turn, causes the bar to bow or curve.

If the thin section isn't too thin, this curve can be taken out by hammering the steel on edge until it is back in line again. Very thin sections, however, can be damaged when forged this way. In these cases, the steel must first be forged into a counter curve. When the bevel is then drawn, the steel bar is straightened at the same time.

Whenever a drawing sequence is completed, it is important that the finished workpiece be free of nicks, cuts, and sharp corners. Check the workpiece carefully, and grind or file out any cracks or nicks that may have developed, no matter how small. Ninety percent of all tool failures start with minor surface flaws like these. As the tool is used, the flaw deepens, eventually causing catastrophic failure.

CUTTING

Blacksmiths do a lot of cold cutting of mild steel but the steels used in tool making are generally too hard or too tough to cut that way. Tool making steels are best cut hot.

The most common cutting operation in tool making is cutting a bar to length. To do this, heat your bar clear through to a light orange heat at the point of the cut, then lay the bar across your hardie and hammer the bar onto the hardie's cutting edge. When the hardie has cut part way through, turn the bar 90°, check to make sure the hardie lines up with your previous cut, and strike several additional blows.

Continue to rotate and hammer the bar until it is nearly cut through, then grip the shorter end of the bar in your vise at the point of the cut and twist the longer piece free. Never cut completely through a bar with your hammer and hardie. This will bring the hammer in contact with the hardie, damaging both.

Slitting is another form of cutting used in tool making. To slit a piece of steel, take a good yellow heat, lay it on the cutting table or cutting plate, and hammer the hot cut along the line of cut, walking the hot cut as you go. This can take a number of heats, depending on the thickness of the steel and the length of the cut.

The claws of claw hammers are slit this way. The inside of the slit is finished with a special, blunt-beveled hot cut that generates the correct inside bevel on each claw.

Bars can also be slit on-end. To do this, heat the bar, clamp it tightly in the vise, and drive your hot cut in to the desired depth.

When slitting a bar only part-way through, it

Here, a hot cut is being used on the anvil's cutting table to trim the end of a skew chisel.

is best, whenever possible, to punch or drill a hole at the termination point of the slit, then cut to the hole. This gives a sound terminus to the cut. Without the hole, there is a strong possibility that a small nick or crack will be left at the end of the slit. This is asking for trouble.

BENDING

Bending is frequently used in tool making. The best place to make a simple bend like a right-angle bend is in the vise.

Heat your piece of steel to a bright orange or yellow at the point of the bend, insert it in the vise, and bend it to the desired shape. If it is a heavy piece of steel, you may have to hammer it to achieve the angle you want.

Most rounded bends can be made on the anvil's horn.

Bending causes a pronounced change in the cross section of a bar because the outside of the bend gets stretched, while the inside of the bend gets compressed. If you want your bend to have the same cross section throughout, you will have to start with a piece of steel that will stretch to the size you want, then hammer down the compressed portion of the bend to match it, truing up the bend as you go.

Bends in tool making steels must always be made at a light orange heat or better. Bending at lower temperatures can cause cracking. Tool makers must also avoid extremely sharp bends. They can also cause cracking.

Bending tapered cross sections on the flat, as when bending inshave blades, causes special problems. Regardless of how well through the bar is heated, the cross section will cup slightly as it is bent. The only way to prevent this is to make these bends between rigid inside and outside forms.

To do this, forge two special forms: one that

Bending a piece of stock over the horn of the anvil.

conforms to the inside of the desired tool, and one that conforms to the outside.

With the inside form clamped securely in a vise, heat the workpiece to a lemon yellow, place it in the form, and hammer the outside form onto it. This will take the cupping out.

Never bend tool making steel over anything with a sharp edge. The edge is sure to cut the steel. Always check the crooks of bends carefully for cracks. File or grind them out completely to avoid grief later on.

PUNCHING

Tool making steels are easily punched by heating them to a bright yellow and driving a punch clear through them with a heavy hammer.

Punching is really a form of cutting; the flat-faced end of the punch shears away some of the steel as it is driven through it.

Keep in mind that a small slug of steel will be cut from the bar as the punch passes through it, and that this slug will drop to the floor when the punch clears the hole. It is a hot little sucker and not something you want to step on.

Small holes can be punched in thin sections in one heat. To make such a hole, first mark its location on the workpiece with a prick punch so you can find the exact spot quickly when the steel's hot.

When the steel is heated clear through, move it to the anvil and start the punch on the anvil's face. When the punch has bitten into the steel, relocate it over the pritchel hole and drive it through.

As soon as the punch clears the steel, it is imperative that you pull or knock it out of the hole as quickly as possible. Steel begins to cool as soon as it leaves the fire, and as it cools, it shrinks. If you don't free your punch quickly, you may not free it at all because the steel will clamp

A traditional eye punch being driven into a work-piece to generate an eye. The heavy sledge speeds the process.

itself onto the punch with surprising tenacity.

Don't be embarrassed if this happens to you the first time out. There are only two kinds of smiths in the world when it comes to punching: Those who have gotten a punch stuck in a workpiece at one time or another, and those who lie and say they haven't.

Larger holes in thicker steel require several heats to complete. To punch such a hole, mark the workpiece with a prick punch as before, heat it to a bright yellow, place it on the anvil, and drive the punch into the workpiece with repeated, heavy blows. When the workpiece cools to an orange heat, quickly remove the punch. Reheat the workpiece and cool the punch in the slack tub.

When the workpiece is properly reheated, remove it from the forge or furnace, and bring it to the anvil. Drop a small lump of coal into the hole you have started before reinserting the punch in the hole and driving it deeper into the steel. The coal will act as a lubricant to help keep the punch from sticking.

Continue this process until the hole is punched three quarters of the way through the bar, then turn the bar over and start the hole from the other side.

How can you be sure that the holes will line up?

Carefully examine the reverse side of the punched bar. You will see that the punch has compressed the steel in front of it so tightly that it has created a dark, polished mark on the surface, called a "rose" in the trade. Carefully place your punch on this mark and drive it home.

Punching causes considerable distortion of the workpiece. While some of the steel in front of the punch is cut, the rest of it is forced aside. This causes the workpiece to swell and lengthen. To correct this distortion, reheat the workpiece to a good yellow heat, reinsert the punch, and hammer the workpiece back into shape, keeping in mind that the punch must be removed periodically so it doesn't get stuck.

Drifting a tool's eye. At left, an eight-pound sledge is used to drift the eye of a small adze. At right, the drift is used to keep the eye shape while the sides of the adze are squared up with a hammer.

FORGING TOOL EYES

In the old days, blacksmiths punched the eyes of their handled tools with an eye-shaped punch.

But there's an easier and better way to forge an eye.

Mark the spot for the eye with a prick punch as before, then take the workpiece to the drill press and drill a pilot hole exactly where you want the eye to be. The new titanium nitride (TiN) coated drills are great for this.

Now heat the workpiece clear through to a bright yellow and generate your eye by driving a drift through the hole you've drilled, enlarging and shaping the hole as you go. The drift will follow the hole <u>exactly</u>. This ensures that the eye is located <u>precisely</u> where you want it, and that it is <u>perfectly perpendicular</u> to the tool head.

By shaping a drift properly and driving it into the hole from both sides, you can generate hourglass-shaped eye sections just like the big guys. You can also forge tapered adze-type eye sections this way.

When making a drift, it's a good idea to size it to match a standard handle. This eliminates

Here the end of a short length of AISI 1095 is being upset on the anvil. The upset portion of the bar will later be forged into a wide gouge blade.

the need for a lot of custom fitting. At Genuine Forgery, all of our drifts are sized to standard handles manufactured by the O.P. Link Handle Co. of Salem, IN (see appendix). Some years ago we tested handles from all of the major American makers, and Link's handles proved superior.

UPSETTING

Upsetting is exactly the opposite of drawing; *it increases the cross section of a bar while shortening it.*

Upsetting, also called jumping, isn't a technique you will use often in tool making, but there are times when creating a large mass at a given point on a bar is desirable.

Upsetting requires a great deal of heat and a lot of force. To upset the end of a bar, heat the end (and end only) to as high a heat as it can possibly stand, then hammer the end of the bar sharply and rapidly. The bar will begin to swell and shorten. When the bar begins to bend out of line, stop upsetting, strike corrective blows, and return the bar to the fire. Repeat this sequence until you have achieved the mass you want.

The middle of a bar can also be upset. Heat the portion of the bar you wish to upset, quickly cool either side of the heated section in the quench tank, then hammer the bar on end, correcting and repeating the sequence as necessary.

There are three keys to successful upsetting. The first is to get the workpiece as hot as it can stand. The second is to keep the heat as localized as possible to avoid a lot of undesirable bending. The third is to correct bending as soon as it occurs.

Upsetting can also be used to develop a constant cross section at a bend. After making the bend, heat the bent section to the highest heat it can stand, then hammer the end of the bar into the bend, massing material there. True up the work as you go.

PACKING

Traditionally, the final step in forging an edge tool is to pack the blade. This involves hammering the entire working end of the blade vigorously and thoroughly at a blood red heat. This hammering compresses the grain or particles that comprise the steel, making it stronger.

FORGE WELDING

In the old days, tool making steel was produced in small batches in crucibles. The resulting cast steel was rare and expensive.

Blacksmiths conserved this scarce commodity by forging their tools from readily available iron, then forge welding or hammer welding small, crucible or cast steel bits onto their working ends.

Over the years, many people have come to believe that this technique produces a superior tool. It doesn't. Tools forged from a single piece of modern tool steel are superior to their forge-welded counterparts. The fact is, forge welding isn't necessary to tool making anymore as excellent tool making steels are readily available in any quantity and at reasonable prices.

SHOP NOTES

Whenever you make a tool, it's a good idea to record its progress in a notebook. Keeping notes helps you remember what does and doesn't work. Write down the size and shape stock you started with and each of the steps you took along the way. These notes will evolve into your own personal handbook on tool making.

A bevel-faced hammer packs the edge of a one-inch cold chisel.

A 50-pound Little Giant power hammer in good working order.

POWER FORGING

Forging a tool can be hard and time consuming work, particularly if the tool has to be made from a large, heavy piece of steel. Blacksmiths have traditionally attacked this problem by employing hammering machines of one type or another to do as much of the bull work as possible.

Buying and installing a large, motor-driven power hammer isn't practical for most woodworkers. But building a small, foot-powered hammer, known as an Oliver or treadle hammer, is a feasible alternative. For $5, ABANA will supply you with plans and a bill of materials for an excellent, foot-operated hammering device that can be made from standard, easily obtained materials. Woodworkers interested in making large tools should give serious consideration to this idea.

Another option is to corral your wife, husband, or friend into working for you as a striker. This was common practice in days past, when smiths employed up to three sledge-wielding assistants or strikers to help draw out large workpieces.

In practice, the striker stands on the other side of the anvil with his or her sledge held at the ready. The striker grips the sledge with hands held 18 to 24-inches apart and never raises the head of the sledge above eye level. This permits the delivery of sharp, accurate blows. The striker should use as large a sledge as he or she is comfortable with; 10 to 12-pounds is a good size for serious drawing out.

When the workpiece is ready for forging, the smith brings the heated steel to the anvil and strikes it once with his own hammer, indicating with this blow where he wants the piece worked. The striker then delivers <u>one</u> heavy blow where indicated. The smith then strikes the next blow, and the striker follows. This continues back and forth until the workpiece has cooled to below forging temperature or the work is done.

Working with a striker usually goes haltingly at first. But in a surprisingly short period of time a natural rhythm develops, and the drawing proceeds with amazing speed and accuracy.

The key to successful team forging is communication. In the old days, blacksmiths used complicated hammer signals to transmit their orders to their helpers. Words were seldom spoken. But for the woodworker turned blacksmith, voice signals work just fine.

Explain beforehand to your striker what you want to accomplish, and continue to give voice instructions as the work proceeds. Simple, direct commands such as "lighter", "more on the edge", and "stop" work best.

It's important to remember that the smith <u>always</u> directs the work. The assistant <u>never</u> strikes a blow unless signaled or told to do so by the smith. This is imperative if striking work is to be carried out safely.

6 FINISHING

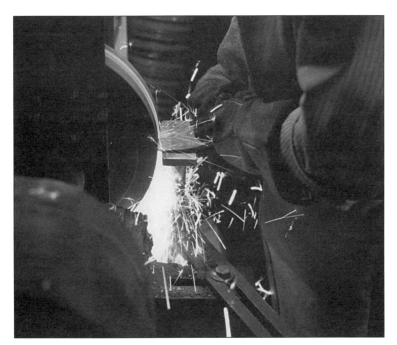

Forging is a technology that can produce a net shape, that is to say, tools can be made from start to finish with forging technology alone.

But this is not the best way to make tools. Over the years, tool makers have come to rely on a combination of technologies, starting with forging and progressing through grinding and finishing, to make tools in the easiest, fastest, and best manner possible.

In the old days, blacksmiths were taught that five minutes at the forge equaled a half-hour at the bench, meaning it is a lot easier to forge a shape than it is to file it. This is still true today. When making a tool, try to forge as close to net shape as possible. But don't be a slave to net shape thinking. Grinding and finishing have a rightful place in tool making, and should be used when appropriate.

This is especially true when forging blades. Blades for woodworking tools should always be forged to near net shape, then finished by grinding to avoid damaging the steel by forging it when it's very thin.

This, too, is an idea that has withstood the test of time; in 1703, when he published his famous <u>Mechanick Exercises</u>, Joseph Moxon recorded this saying of the ancient English edge-tool makers:

"He that will a good Edge win, Must Forge thick and Grind thin."

When a tool has been forged as near to net shape as practical, it is time for finishing.

Preliminary finishing is used to get the tool ready for heat treatment. This is the time to grind, file and sand out any imperfections, and to fine-tune the rough-forged tool to exactly the size and shape you want.

The first step in preliminary finishing is usually grinding.

GRINDING

In the old days, tool makers used giant, hand-cut grinding wheels quarried from natural stone to perform all of their grinding chores.

Grinding has come a long way in the years since. Modern grinding wheels are produced from man-made abrasive materials custom formulated to specific applications, and the modern grinders they run on are capable of much higher speeds than their doddering ancestors. Metal removal rates are incredible.

SELECTING A GRINDER

A small, modern bench grinder can provide all the grinding power you need.

Grinding efficiency is in direct proportion to surface speed, so select a 3/4 HP or better double-end grinder that will comfortably turn 8-inch to 10-inch wheels at a minimum of 3450 RPMs. A 220-V unit is preferable. Baldor and Wilton are two names to look for, and their machines are available new or used in all the

The gap between the tool rest and the grinding wheel must never exceed ⅛ inch.

The correct, balanced stance for grinding or dressing the wheel.

usual places.

You will need two grades of grinding wheels. For rough work, use a medium grain, aluminum oxide vitrified wheel with good hardness such as Norton Abrasives' A36-S5V type. Norton, based in Worcester, MA, is the world's leading producer of grinding wheels, and everybody speaks their language. For finishing work and general tool sharpening, use a finer grained, aluminum oxide vitrified wheel that is somewhat softer, such as Norton's A60-M5V type.

Grinding wheel designations can be confusing. Don't worry about the numbers. Just use wheels comparable to the types mentioned here and you'll be fine.

I have done a lot of serious production grinding over the years on wheels made by a dozen or so different companies. Norton and Carborundum Co. wheels are consistently excellent, but I really haven't seen much difference in performance amongst any of the brands. A lot of the imported stuff is pretty good.

To get the most oomph for your grind, keep your wheels clean and dressed. Get yourself a Huntington #1 wheel dresser and a box of replacement cutters. Use the dresser often. They are available from Wholesale Tool and other industrial suppliers. Diamond dressers are also effective, but they're expensive.

Regardless of what you are grinding, always keep the tool rest as close as possible to the wheel. The gap between the two should never exceed ⅛-inch.

When buying wheels, try to match the hole size of the wheel to the arbor of your grinder exactly. Never try to enlarge the center hole of a wheel to fit your grinder. If the center hole is larger than your arbor, use factory-made bushings designed specifically for the job.

Make sure your wheels are faced on both sides with blotter paper. The paper is there to protect the wheel from cracking due to uneven flange pressure. Never use a wheel without placing pieces of blotter paper between the wheel and the grinder's flanges.

GRINDING TOOLS

There are no hard and fast rules as to what comes first in finishing. Each tool is unique and has its own best finishing sequence. Generally speaking, the first step in finishing is grinding to shape. Use this step to clean up and perfect the lines of the tool, and to eliminate any nicks or sharp edges that developed during forging.

The next step is usually grinding to size. This requires good, industrial-grade measuring tools. To do it right, you should have a 30-inch, stainless steel rule that can also serve as a straight edge, a 6-inch stainless steel rule that can also serve as a straight edge, a stainless steel protractor, a good vernier caliper (the Sears version is fine), and a good combination square. The vernier caliper can also be used as a sizing gauge when drawing.

A 6-inch by 48-inch belt sander generates the bevel on a mortising chisel. The belt sander is extremely useful for generating flat surfaces like this. For safety's sake, the sander should be rigged to drive the belt counterclockwise or up and away from the operator, rather than down and toward the operator.

SANDING

After grinding, it's a good idea to run your tool past a stationary belt sander to clean up any sharp edges that remain from forging and grinding. My 6-inch by 48-inch machine is an old Sears model. It runs fine and is perfectly suited to this work. The bearings go on it every other year, but they're easily replaced.

For general finishing and shaping work, use a 60-grit aluminum oxide cloth belt. You can get these for $2.40 apiece in quantity from Enco Manufacturing Co. (see appendix). They're not as good as a $10.19 Norton zirconia alumina belt, but they're good enough to be more cost

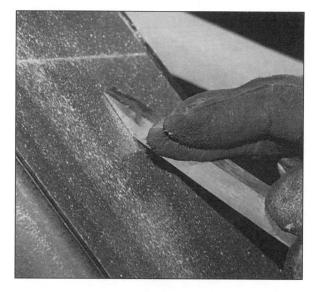

effective than the expensive Norton belt over the long haul.

If you don't have a sanding machine, a portable belt sander clamped firmly in a vise works almost as well.

FILING

Even when I am making tools in quantity, say 200 at a time, I always take each tool to the bench after grinding and sanding to complete the shaping and sizing process by hand. Clamp the tool in a good, industrial-grade machinist's vise that is well lighted, and file finish the tool all over.

Smooth-cut files work best for this operation. You will need 6-inch, 10-inch and 16-inch round files, 10-inch and 16-inch square files, and a 16-inch to 20-inch flat file. Over the years I have found that inexpensive imported files are more cost effective than top-of-the-line American brands.

Filing is an art in its own right. Here are some tips to help you develop your filing skills:

Always fit a file handle to the file you are using. It will save wear and tear on your hand. It will also improve your power and accuracy. A sharp file in the hands of a good workman is capable of serious metal removal. It is the poor man's milling machine.

Set yourself solidly with feet planted shoulder length apart. This will give you good balance. Grip the file handle in one hand and the tip of the file in the other to get good control and maximum power. Filing is a two-handed operation.

Always lift the file just off the workpiece on the return stroke. This will keep the file sharp longer. Dragging the file back over the work tends to

The proper stance for filing. Feet are planted solidly, shoulder length apart, and the file is held in two hands.

dull and even break off a file's cutting teeth.

Clean your file frequently. To clean a file, first rap the tip sharply against the side of the vise. This will jar a lot of the filings loose. Next, run a file card over the file's cutting surfaces. Finally, use a sharp nail or similar device to pry off any stickers that remain wedged in the file's teeth. These stickers can cause the file to skip over the work.

Replace your files regularly. One of the biggest mistakes beginning smiths make is trying to get too much work out of dull tools such as files and hacksaw blades. And steer clear of the various file reconditioning services. They cost more than they're worth.

When your filing work is complete, go over your tool with a piece of 60-or 120-grit aluminum oxide coated abrasive.

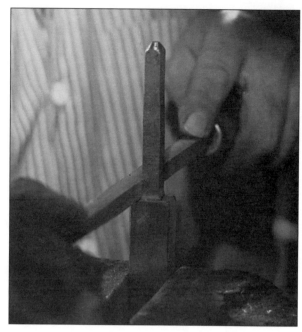

A good, square-shaped smooth file makes quick work of truing the shoulder on a mortising chisel.

FLAT SURFACES

Tools like chisels and plane irons require perfectly flat backs to work well. When drawing a tool like this, be sure to use your flatter liberally, and check the finished forging for flatness with your straight edge. This is one of those instances where a few minutes at the forge can save a lot of time finishing.

The 6-inch by 48-inch belt sander is ideally suited to generating flat surfaces. Make a quick pass on the machine, then check the piece carefully under a good light to see how close your forging is to flat. If you see a number of deep, unsanded depressions, reforge for smoothness; it's a lot faster than sanding all that steel away.

When flattening a tool on the belt sander, start with a 36-grit Norton or Hermes zirconia alumina belt. They're expensive, but they can really cut. Complete the tool on a worn, 60-grit belt for a good finish.

A portable belt sander clamped firmly in a vise can be used for this job as well.

DECARBURIZATION

Most tool making steels rely on high carbon content for hardness, but some of this carbon is driven out of the surface of steel during forging. This thin, oxidized surface, approximately .010 to .020 inches deep, must be ground away if the tool is to be hardened successfully.

Because you will be grinding all of your bevels, decarburization isn't a problem on the bevel side of the tool.

But don't forget the back of the blade or bevel. This, too, has been decarburized, and must be ground both to remove any surface blemishes from forging and to remove all decarburized material.

GRINDING BEVELS

Bevels can be cut on the grinder, sander, or both. I usually find myself roughing out a bevel on the grinder, dressing it on the sander, and finishing it at the bench with a smooth-cut file and bench stone.

Don't try to get the edge too sharp at this stage. Until they're heat treated, even the best tool making steels break down when sharpened too finely.

Concentrate instead on getting a consistent bevel across the entire length of the blade. This will insure that the tool will cut uniformly when it is heat treated and sharpened.

Grinding a consistent bevel, particularly a long bevel, as on a draw knife, takes practice. This is especially true when doing hollow grinding.

The grinder is ideal for roughing out bevels. Remember to brace the work solidly on the grinder's tool rest to prevent the tool from catching and flying out of your hands while you're working.

HOLLOW GRINDING

Hollow grinding is the art of grinding a concave bevel or cutting edge. Hollow-ground edges have become very popular with woodworkers in recent years because it's easier to maintain a keen edge on them.

The concave surface of a hollow-ground edge is generated by the radius of the grinding wheel, but it takes a steady hand to cut a hollow edge freehand. In fact, the easiest and best way to grind a hollow edge is to clamp your blade in an angled fixture that slides along your grinder's tool rest. The fixture helps maintain a constant angle of presentation to the grinding wheel.

FINAL FINISHING

After a tool is heat treated, there is still some finishing work to be done. The first step is usually polishing.

POLISHING

Heat treating leaves a tool discolored. It will work perfectly well that way, but most woodworkers want their tools, especially the backs and cutting edges, polished to a high finish.

There is no magic solution here. As in woodworking, the quality of the surface is in direct proportion to the amount of elbow grease applied thereto. Start with 120-grit coated and take it is as far as you want to go.

I find large flap wheels mounted on a mandrel to be a very effective way of getting a good finish fast.

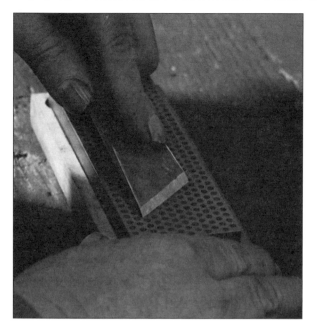

A diamond-type bench stone being used to sharpen a bevel, above. The tool should be checked periodically against a protractor, as below, to assure that the correct angle is being maintained.

SHARPENING

Your heat treated tool also needs to be sharpened. Sharpening a tool on progressively harder natural Arkansas stones and finishing with a little compound on the buffing wheel still gives the best cutting edge. But it's slow going.

In the interest of production, start with a coarse diamond stone, roughing down to as fine as possible, then finish off with medium and fine water stones and the buffing wheel.

Water stones are good cutters, but they hollow out quickly and require frequent flattening. The new ceramic stones are much better in this regard, requiring no maintenance save occasional cleaning. Unfortunately, they're slower than water stones.

The single, biggest problem I have seen in sharpening is rounding over of the cutting edge. This comes from inadvertently rocking the tool on the stone during sharpening.

Rounding over the cutting edge does all kinds of bad things to it. It increases the angle of the cutting edge, lowering its efficiency. It alters the rake angle, or angle of attack, making the tool difficult or impossible to use correctly. It also impedes development of a clean, flowing chip, reducing the quality of the cut and increasing the amount of force needed to move the tool through the work.

Use your protractor under a good light to carefully check your bevels. If they show signs of rounding, get yourself one of the many high-quality honing guides now on the market. Used properly, they can eliminate rocking and help you generate really good edges.

HANDLING

You can put a handle on a tool in less than a minute but before you know it, it's rattling around and driving you crazy. Take the time needed to do the job right. You'll be rewarded with <u>years</u> of trouble-free service.

HANDLING STRIKING TOOLS

Most lightweight striking or impact tools used in woodworking have hourglass-shaped eye sections. That is to say, the openings are slightly larger at the top and bottom of the section than they are in the middle of the section.

To handle this type of tool, select a handle with a cross section a hair larger than the opening of the eye.

Heat the end of the handle for a half-hour at around 125°F to drive out any ambient moisture it contains. A kitchen oven does this job well.

When the handle is as dry as you can get it, drive it onto the head of the tool. As the handle is driven into the eye, the eye's narrower midsection will compress the outer fibers of the wood. These fibers will spring back as the handle is driven all the way home, locking the tool head in place.

When the handle has been driven onto the tool as tightly as possible, clamp it right side up in the vise, and apply a liberal dose of swelling compound such as Chair-Lok to the wedge slot and the end of the handle. Then drive the wooden wedge into the slot as deeply as it will go. Trim off any excess handle that sticks up beyond the top of the tool with a fine-toothed saw, then finish by driving in a steel wedge 45 degrees to the wooden wedge. This handle will not loosen for years.

Tools with adze-type eye sections, that is to say, eye sections that taper uniformly from a

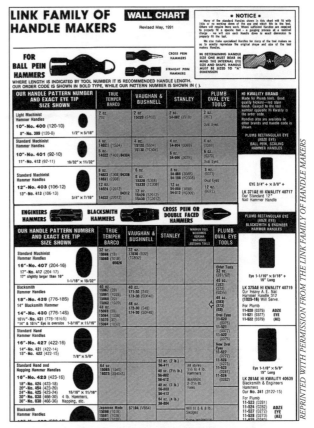

This is a sample of the wall chart available from the O.P. Link Handle Co., which shows some of the handle types they supply. See the appendix for information on contacting them.

REPRINTED WITH PERMISSION FROM THE LINK FAMILY OF HANDLE MAKERS

small hole at the bottom of the tool to a larger hole at the top of the tool, do not employ wooden or steel wedges. Rather, the handle is inserted through the top of the tool and driven home. The taper locks the tool in place during use, but allows you to drive the tool off when it requires sharpening. This is a convenience in some tools and a necessity in others, such as adzes, whose cutting edges are difficult or impossible to reach with the handle in place.

HANDLING DRAWN TOOLS

Drawknives, inshaves, and other drawn tools have traditionally been handled by locking the tang over the back of the handle. This involves drilling a hole completely through the handle, then forcing the heated tang of the tool through the hole and beyond. The hot, protruding tang end is then bent or hammered over the end of the handle. The handle is then cooled in the slack tub to prevent the heated tang from burning it up.

Old-time blacksmiths used this method because the tang burns itself onto the wood, making for a tight seat, and the peened-over tang end locks the handle tightly in place.

The big disadvantage of this method becomes apparent when a handle needs to be replaced. The bent tang must be heated and forged straight again before a new handle can be affixed. Often the bent length of tang breaks during handle removal, necessitating reforging as well as refitting.

A better way to handle these tools is to epoxy them. Ream a tapered hole $3^{1}/_{2}$-inches to 4-inches deep in each handle. Pour equal amounts of epoxy and hardener into the hole, mix thoroughly with a splinter of wood, and press the tang into the hole. Let set overnight.

Genuine Forgery has been doing this for

When the epoxy and hardener have been thoroughly mixed in the handle hole, the handle for this combination drawknife can be seated.

about ten years now on all of its drawn tools. There has not been a single report of failure in all that time. For best results, use Devcon 5-Minute Epoxy, an industrial type epoxy designed to bond wood and metal, which you can get at the hardware store.

HANDLING CHISELS

Chisels are easy to handle. Bore a hole that will accept the tool's tang, then clamp the tool firmly in a vise and drive the handle onto it until it rests firmly against the tool's bolster.

If the chisel doesn't have a bolster, file a stop in the tang and place a washer between the stop and the handle to act as a bolster. This trick, developed by artist/tool maker Alex Weygers, will prevent the tang from being driven deeper into the handle and splitting it open during use.

Some carvers place a leather washer between the handle and the bolster of all carving tools that are struck with a mallet. They say it prolongs the life of the handle and reduces the shock to the hand holding the tool.

When making chisels, forge the tangs square so the tool doesn't turn in the handle. For standard woodworking chisels, including carving chisels, a 1/4-inch square tang 3 inches long is sufficient. Drill a 9/32-inch hole in your handle to accept this tang. For heavier chisels, forge a 5/16-inch square tang 3-inches long and drill a 3/8-inch hole for the handle. For super-duty tools like boatbuilder's slicks, forge a 3/8-inch square tang 3-inches long and drill a 7/16-inch hole for the handle.

With a washer-type bolster held in place, the handle for this skew chisel is driven home.

7 HEAT TREATING

Heat treating is the single most misunderstood aspect of tool making. More erroneous information has been circulated on the subject than any other. And yet, as with every other aspect of tool making, heat treating is comprised of a few basic elements that are easily understood and readily mastered.

Many of the problems people have with heat treating can be traced to improper use of heat treating terminology. Hardening, annealing, tempering, and other heat treating terms have <u>precise</u> meanings. Yet they are often used incorrectly. This has created a great deal of misunderstanding among beginning tool makers and a lot of ruined tools.

HEAT TREATING DEFINED

For our purposes, heat treating may be defined as <u>any</u> application and/or manipulation of heat to develop specific properties in tool making steels.

Three basic processes are involved:

ANNEALING

This is the process of softening and/or stress relieving steel after it has been forged, heavily machined, or previously heat treated.

HARDENING

This is the process of heating tool making steels to temperatures that trigger the formation of extremely hard carbides within their structures. These carbides are then frozen in place by quenching the steel or rapidly reducing its temperature.

TEMPERING

Steel that has been hardened by quenching is too hard and brittle to do work. It must be carefully reheated to dissolve some of the carbides formed during hardening. This makes the steel somewhat softer, and tough enough to do work without breaking. This reheating process is called tempering.

CRITICAL TEMPERATURE

Before you can perform any heat treating operation on a piece of tool making steel, you need to know the steel's critical temperature, or the temperature above which the steel will harden. Every heat treating operation you will be called upon to perform is based on critical temperature. This temperature, differs somewhat from steel to steel.

For high carbon steels, including W-1, W-2, and W-4 tool steels, the critical temperature is 1350°F.

It's easy to tell when high carbon steel reaches its critical temperature: It loses its magnetism.

Thus, since time immemorial, smiths have judged the critical temperature of high carbon

High carbon steel loses its magnetism when its critical temperature is reached.

Steel	Critical Temperature	Color
O-1	1370° F	Cherry
D-2	1490° F	Very Bright Cherry
A-2	1460° F	Bright Cherry
M-2	1530° F	Salmon
M-42	1560° F	Salmon
S-5	1400° F	Strong Cherry

steel by heating it slowly and periodically touching a magnet to it. At the moment the steel loses its magnetism, it has reached its critical temperature. This also works for the alloy steels discussed earlier.

Judging the critical temperatures of other tool making steels isn't as easy because a magnet won't indicate when their critical temperature has been reached. Thus, the tool maker must estimate the steel's critical temperature by the incandescent color it exhibits as it is heated (see color chart).

It is impossible to estimate the critical temperature of a piece of steel <u>exactly</u> this way. But with a little patience and perseverance, you'll be able to come close enough to get excellent results.

The chart to the left gives the critical temperature of the remaining tool making steels discussed in Chapter 1 of this book, along with the incandescent color these steels exhibit when they reach critical temperature.

Keep in mind that these colors are subject to interpretation and will change somewhat in different lights. Experiment. Make notes. If you're not getting good results, try a little more or a little less heat until you get what you're looking for.

FORGE VS. FURNACE

Forges and furnaces are both effective sources of heat for heat treating tools.

Furnaces develop a large, even, penetrating heat that is very useful when working with large, heavy, and long tools. But it's hard to contain all that heat. Sometimes as a result, you have to harden more of a tool than you'd like.

Forges, on the other hard, develop an excellent local heat that allows you to do localized heat treating. That is to say, you can harden a small portion of a tool while leaving the rest of the tool soft and very tough. Because the unhardened portion of the tool is resistant to breaking, you can leave the edge harder than you might if the entire tool or blade had to be hardened.

ANNEALING

The most common heat treating operation performed by tool makers is annealing.

Tool making steels have complex internal structures. Forging and machining these steels has two effects upon them. First, it hardens them somewhat, making it difficult to file or otherwise finish them. Second, it creates internal stresses in them which must be relieved. It is good practice, therefore, to anneal your steel after each forging or heavy machining sequence.

Annealing is also performed to prepare a tool for hardening; <u>always</u> anneal a tool before attempting to harden it.

To anneal a workpiece, heat it clear through to <u>just above</u> its critical temperature, then cool it very slowly.

The most common way to cool steel slowly is to bury it in a large container of ashes, sand, or slaked lime. These materials hold the heat in the steel and retard the cooling rate. This practice works on all of the steels discussed in Chapter 1 of this book, with these exceptions:

O-1
Heat uniformly to 1450°F (Bright Cherry), hold at that heat for two hours, cool slowly in the fire to 1200°F (just under Medium Cherry), then remove from the fire and air cool to room temperature.

D-2
Heat uniformly to 1650°F (Very Dark Orange), hold at that temperature for two hours, cool slowly in the fire to 1200°F (just under Medium Cherry), then remove from fire and air cool.

A-2

Heat uniformly to 1600°F (Bright Salmon), hold at that temperature for two hours, cool slowly in the fire to 1400°F (just under Bright Cherry), then allow to cool slowly overnight in fire.

M-2, M-42

Heat uniformly to 1600°F (Bright Salmon), hold at that heat for two hours, cool slowly in the fire to 1175°F (Dark Cherry), then remove from the fire and air cool.

S-5

Heat uniformly to 1425°F (just under Bright Cherry), hold at that heat for two hours, cool slowly in the fire to 1175°F (Dark Cherry), then remove from the fire and air cool.

ANNEALING PREVIOUSLY HARDENED STEEL

When working with a piece of steel that has already been hardened, such as an old spring, it is essential that you anneal the steel thoroughly before attempting to do anything with it.

The annealing procedures for previously hardened steel are the same as they are for new steel, with one exception: It is extremely important to heat the steel very slowly and very thoroughly to its annealing temperature to avoid damaging it.

This is equally true when reworking previously hardened tools. The initial heat you take on these tools must be slow and even to avoid cracking.

FLOOR ANNEALING

For a few tools that require a great deal of toughness with only moderate hardness, such as wrecking and pry bars, the recommended heat treatment procedure is simply to lay the tool on the shop floor to cool when forging has been completed. This is known in the trade as floor annealing.

This also works for some heavy springs, such as blacksmith's vise springs.

NORMALIZING

Normalizing is an abbreviated form of annealing that can be used with high carbon and oil-hardening steels. It is not a substitute for annealing and should only be used between forging sequences.

For example, if you are forging a tool and must interrupt forging operations before you are finished, normalizing will satisfactorily relieve any internal stresses that have developed up to that point.

To normalize a tool, heat it clear through to 1600°F (Bright Salmon), then set it aside to air cool.

Remember, normalizing can only be used on high carbon and oil-hardening steels. It can <u>not</u> be used with high speed, air hardening, or shock-resisting steels.

HARDENING

Hardening is the heat treating operation performed to harden the working part of a tool to enable it to perform work.

The edges of cutting tools are hardened to enable them to take and hold a keen edge. The faces of striking tools, such as hammers, are hardened to allow their striking surfaces to do work without deforming or otherwise spoiling.

To harden a piece of high carbon steel, or a

piece of W-1, W-2, W-4, oil-hardening, or S-5 tool steel, heat it slowly and clear through to <u>just slightly higher</u> than its critical temperature, then quench or rapidly cool it in the appropriate medium.

It is important not to overheat your steel. If you do overheat a piece of steel at this point, do not attempt to harden it. This will damage the steel and a poor tool will result. Instead, lay it aside on a bed of ashes and let it cool to room temperature before trying again.

Technique is important in quenching. Chisels, hammers, and other tools heated on one end should be plunged straight down into the quench tank. Long blades, like knife blades, should be plunged into the tank with the blade parallel to the surface of the medium. This will help prevent twisting or distorting of the workpiece.

As soon as the tool is plunged into the medium, it's important to agitate it rapidly and continuously. This prevents the formation of steam around the blade, which can act as a barrier between the blade and the medium, preventing the medium from reaching the blade and doing its job.

When the quenching medium has reduced the temperature of the heated edge or face to 150°F, remove it from the medium and lay it on a bed of ashes to cool to room temperature. You know you've hit 150°F when you can just touch a tool but can't keep your finger on it.

When hardening double-ended tools, always do the heaviest end first. Temper this end, then wrap it in a soaking wet rag to prevent it from being overheated while you're heat treating the other end.

DELICATE TOOLS

Thin and delicate tools require a slightly different technique. With these tools, heat a heavy block of steel at least 1-inch thick to a yellow heat, place it on a refractory brick on the anvil, and use the heat radiating from the steel block to heat the tool to the correct hardening temperature. This technique gives a great deal more control over the heating process. Quench as above.

QUENCHING MEDIUMS

For most high carbon steels, including W-1, W-2, and W-4 tool steels, a large tub of slack or soft water is a satisfactory quench medium. It's important that it be a large tub so there is enough mass to pull the heat from the tool quickly. This is the key to hardening: the heat must be pulled from the tool rapidly in order for it to harden properly.

When hardening hammers and other striking tools, float a thin layer of light machine oil on the surface of the quench water. This retards the cooling effect of the quench water slightly, improving the toughness of the hammer face. The faces of hammers quenched in plain water tend to gall after they have been used for a while because they work harden in use and become somewhat brittle.

When hardening very thin sections, and curved blades like gouges and inshaves, light machine oil is the preferred medium. The light oil cools the tool rapidly enough for hardening to take place, but reduces thermal and mechanical shock to safe levels.

O-1 and S-5 tool steels are best quenched in medium-weight quench oil. Used crank case oil also does a good job on these steels.

Special care must be taken when quenching in oil as the oil can burst into flame from the heat of the tool, causing severe burns. Keep your hands and face away from the opening of the oil bath. Always <u>immerse the tool completely</u> so that no part of it breaks the surface of the quenchant. Keep a strong, tight-fitting lid handy. Placing it over the bath will quickly smother any fire that breaks out.

For engraving tools and the like which must have the hardest edges possible, brine is the quench medium of choice. The addition of salt to the water reduces its tendency to boil and steam around the blade. This allows the water to pull the heat from the blade faster.

You can make a satisfactory brine quench by adding rock salt to a container of water until the water is so saturated it won't take more. Brine is nasty, corrosive stuff. Use an industrial-strength, plastic container for your brine quench; it eats up just about everything else.

AIR-HARDENING STEEL

Air-hardening steels like D-2 and A-2 are hardened differently.

To harden A-2 and D-2 steel, heat slowly to 1800°F (lemon), let the heat soak in thoroughly, then set aside to cool slowly in still air. When the steel has cooled to 150°F, reheat to 1100°F (dull red), and set aside again to cool in still air. This is known as the double hardening method.

An alternative method is to heat these steels to 1800°F (lemon), quench in oil until temperature has dropped to 1100°F (dull red), then set aside to cool in still air. This is known as the interrupted quench method.

The two methods work equally well. Choose the one that works best for you.

HIGH SPEED STEEL

To harden high speed steels like M-2 and M-42, heat the steel thoroughly to 1550°F (salmon), bring it rapidly to 2200°F (a white fusing heat), then quench in oil and set aside to cool in still air.

An alternative method is to heat as above, remove from the fire and cool in a blast of cold air. The steel will not get quite as hard this way, but will have considerably more toughness.

Use a spare blower or the blower from your forge or furnace to provide the blast of air.

OXIDATION PROTECTION

Heating tool making steels to hardening temperatures causes considerable scaling or oxidation. Some smiths avoid this by first dipping the steel into a heated solution of common borax and water. As the borax solution dries, it forms a thin, protective coating on the steel, preventing oxidation.

Another solution is to wrap your steel tightly in one of the protective foil products specially made for this purpose. Ticronic Tool Steel Foil Wrap, manufactured by Shop-Aid Co., Boston, is a widely available wrap that is reliable.

The use of these oxidation protection measures has its down side; it's very difficult to judge the hardening temperature of steels that are so protected. Because of this, these measures are best used with furnaces equipped with temperature recording devices.

TEMPERING

When tool making steels have been properly hardened, they are too hard to put to use, that is to say, their edges and/or faces are so hard they are brittle. These edges and faces must be tempered or drawn somewhat to increase their toughness.

Some tools require more hardness than others. Carving chisels, for example, need to be quite hard in order to take and hold a very keen edge. But this keenness of edge comes at a price: The harder an edge is, the more brittle it is.

Other tools, likes axes and adzes, need more toughness than hardness to do their work well.

The dilemma, then, that the heat treater faces when tempering tools is to decide how hard he or she can leave a tool while developing the necessary level of toughness in it.

There is no single, correct solution to this question. Each tool maker/user must arrive at the solution that works best for him or her. A careful, respectful user can make his or her chisel a lot harder than the person who plans to use it occasionally to pry open paint cans.

TEMPERING TECHNIQUES

Tempering, known in the old days as coloring the steel, must be done immediately after hardening. Hardening imparts considerable strain in a tool that must be relieved.

To temper high carbon, W-1, W-2, and W-4 tool steel, and O-1 and S-5 tool steels, lightly polish the hardened end to a bright finish on your sander, then heat the polished portion of the tool evenly with a common propane torch. Concentrate the flame on the polished portion furthest from the edge. Do not dwell on the edge.

Periodically remove the flame from the tool to slow the heating process. It's important to heat the steel slowly and evenly.

Keep a close eye on the blade. After a time, determined by the heat of the flame and the size of the section, the polished steel will begin to take on an extremely pale, yellowish hue.

Immediately remove the flame from the steel at this point to let the color stabilize. Then apply additional heat in small amounts. The pale, yellowish hue will slowly evolve into faint straw, followed by straw, deep straw, bronze, peacock, deep blue, and light blue. Each of these colors signifies that the heated tool end has reached a certain temperature and has, in the process, experienced a reduction in hardness

Tempering a carver's skew chisel with a propane torch.

Color	Temperature	Tools
Faint Straw	400° F	Burnishers
Straw	440° F	Gravers, scratch awls, some carving tools, floats
Deep Straw	475° F	Knives, carving tools, some turning tools, chisels, hammers, plane irons, gouges, spoke shave and travisher blades, routers
Bronze	520° F	Augers, drills, reamers, heavy turning tools
Peacock	540° F	Drawknives, inshaves, scorps, block knives, hollowing shaves, shears, gimlets
Full Blue	590° F	Heavy axes and adzes, screwdrivers, froes, wedges
Light Blue	640° F	Too soft for woodworking tools

and a corresponding increase in toughness.

When the steel reaches the color you're looking for, plunge it into the slack tub and agitate it vigorously to freeze the steel's structure at that point.

How far you take a given tool is up to you, the chart above outlines some general guidelines developed over the years at Genuine Forgery.

Suggestions for tempering some common woodworking tools.

TEMPERING AIR HARDENING STEEL

Air hardening steels should be drawn to a peacock, set aside to cool to room temperature, then drawn again to a full peacock. This is called *double tempering*. Some smiths use this on all of the tool steels, believing that it further stabilizes the structure of the steel.

TEMPERING HIGH SPEED STEEL

High speed steel that has been quenched in oil has an extremely broad tempering range. For maximum hardness, draw to a faint straw. If this proves too brittle, increase the draw temperature up to blood red on the incandescent color scale.

High speed steel quenched in air often doesn't require tempering. That's because air quenching is less radical than oil quenching, and imparts much less stress in the tool.

HEAT TREATING THE ALLOY STEELS

To heat treat SAE/AISI 52100 alloy steel, follow the same procedures as for high carbon steel.

As noted earlier, the rest of the alloy steels discussed in Chapter 1 of this book should be used only when higher quality steels are unavailable.

To heat treat these steels, follow the guidelines for high carbon steel but quench in oil, not water.

No tempering is required for most woodworking applications.

COLD TREATING

Metallurgists have known for some time that the hardness of tool making steels can be increased by subjecting tools that have been hardened and tempered conventionally to sub-zero temperatures, once the tools have reached room temperature. Most industrial heat treaters perform this operation in special refrigeration units capable of reaching -70°F.

Modern knife makers claim they can successfully duplicate this process by packing a hardened and tempered knife blade in dry ice for several hours. It is a trick worth trying if you absolutely need to get the maximum hardness possible for a particular application.

Remember, however, that tools subjected to

this treatment must be re-tempered in the conventional manner before they can be put to use.

TEMPILSTIKS

Throughout the heat treating section, emphasis has been placed on judging the temperature of steel by reading the incandescent colors it displays as it is heated.

Beginning smiths often find this difficult. A good alternative is to use temperature-indicating crayons. These markers, known by the trade name Tempilstiks, are available from Centaur Forge and other supply houses.

Each Tempilstik is designed to melt at a specific temperature. More than 100 are available covering a range of from 100°F to 2500°F. Accuracy is said to be plus or minus one percent of a crayon's rating.

WORK HARDENING

When any metal is subjected to repeated hammering at room temperature, the molecules that make up the metal become more compressed, and the spaces between the molecules become smaller. As a result, the metal gets harder. This phenomenon is known as *work hardening*.

In ancient times, before the smelting of iron, smiths routinely cold worked the blades of copper and bronze tools to increase their hardness and thus, their ability to hold a keen edge.

Work hardening, however, is not a technique smiths should employ when making modern, steel tools. Work hardening can increase the hardness of steel edges, but it also imparts stresses in the metal that can cause the tool to fail either during work hardening or in service.

Work hardening can cause other problems as well. Tests conducted at Old Sturbridge Village in 1980 showed that the faces of anvils, normally tempered to around 55 on the Rockwell C scale, can work harden to as high as 72 on the Rockwell C scale after many years of hard service. This is a major cause of anvil failure. The face becomes so embrittled by repeated hammering that it eventually chips, spalls, cracks, or breaks away from the body.

Work embrittlement happens to forging hammers as well, and the wise smith retempers his hammers periodically to relieve some of the stresses that have built up in them over time.

HOW HARD IS HARD?

Blacksmiths have traditionally judged the hardness of steel by working it with new and worn files. They can tell from experience how hard a piece of steel is, based on how well these files do and don't mark or cut into the steel.

Beginning tool makers find this to be one of the hardest skills to master.

If you want to take a short cut here, get hold of a set of hardness testing files. These files, manufactured by Tsubosan of Japan, are available from Travers Tool and other industrial suppliers.

The set contains six files precisely hardened and tempered to increasing degrees of hardness, starting from 40 to 42 on the Rockwell C scale, and increasing from 64 to 66 on the Rockwell C scale. By using these files on a piece of hardened steel, you can reliably quantify its hardness, starting from a low of 40 on the Rockwell C scale, and rising to 65 on the Rockwell C scale.

These file sets aren't cheap, but they have the added advantage of recording hardness in Rockwell C-talk, the common language of tool hardness.

A set of Tsubosan hardness files being used to check the edge hardness of a chairmaker's saddling gouge.

CASE HARDENING

Case hardening is the practice of coating soft or mild steel with a commercially prepared compound, then heating the steel to a specified temperature. The heat allows the steel to absorb the compound, thereby hardening its case or surface.

Case hardening does not produce a long-lasting tool, but works in a pinch and is good for one-shot tools.

Kasenit Surface Hardening Compound, manufactured by Kasenit Co., Mahwah, NJ, is a good, reliable case hardening agent. It is available from many industrial suppliers. Follow the directions on the label.

Note: Kasenit is safe and non-poisonous. This is <u>not true</u> with many of the older case-hardening compounds, which contain cyanide and require careful handling.

INNOVATIVE HEAT TREATING

If you're faced with the problem of heat treating a tool that can't be done in a forge or a furnace, don't be afraid to innovate.

Some years ago, when I was developing scythe-making technology for Old Sturbridge Village, I was faced with the need to harden and temper 42-inch long grain cradle blades. To accomplish the task, I threw up a long, narrow forge of cinder blocks on the concrete floor, laid a 2-inch pipe full of holes down the middle of it, and connected the pipe to a hand-cranked blower. Using coke for fuel, I was able to heat treat these blades without a hitch.

8 MAKING A CARVER'S SKEW CHISEL

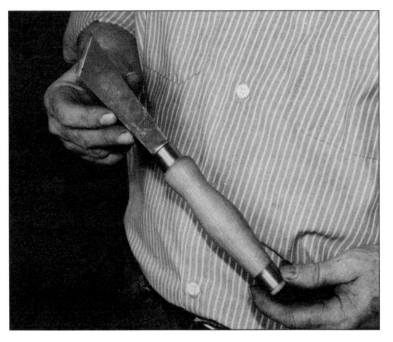

Now that the basic elements of tool making have been discussed in detail, it's time to make some tools.

The carver's skew chisel is a good place to start. It's a relatively easy tool to make, but will teach you a lot about drawing out, and about forging tangs and tapers.

The skew chisel is a mainstay in the woodcarver's arsenal. It takes its name from the fact that its blade is skewed or angled, rather than perpendicular, to the tool's centerline.

The skew chisel is used principally for getting into corners that cannot be reached with standard or straight chisels and gouges. Because of this it is also sometimes called a corner chisel. The skew chisel is also used for lining and fine detailing work.

The chisel we are making here has a 1¹/₂-inch wide blade. This is about as big as carvers' skew chisels get. It is designed for heavy work on large carvings and is fitted with a double-hooped handle. This allows the carver to drive it with a mallet.

The cutting edge of our chisel is skewed 60° to the tool's centerline. This is a good, standard angle, but many carvers prefer to have several skew chisels with different angles to handle different situations.

Our skew chisel also has a 25° double bevel, but this angle is somewhat arbitrary. In practice, the correct bevel angle ranges from 20° to 30°, depending on how the tool is to be used and on what type wood it is to be used.

FORGING THE BLADE

The blank for our skew chisel blade is a piece of 1-inch by ¼-inch AISI 1095 high carbon steel 5 inches long. Other sizes and shapes of blanks with the same volume of steel in them could also be used, but this blank gives us an opportunity to do a lot of drawing out, the most basic of forging techniques.

To begin the tool, grip the blank tightly in an appropriately sized pair of tongs. Place the blank in the forge or furnace (a forge is being used here), and heat approximately 2 inches of one end of the blank to a light yellow. Remember when heating this blank for the first time to soak it for 20 to 30 seconds to get a through heat.

Set the heated end of the blank on a fuller mounted in the hardie hole or blacksmith's vise, and hammer indentations into both edges, setting off approximately one inch for the tool's tang.

Reheat the tool and begin drawing out a ¼-inch square tang. It will take several heats to forge the tang out to its full length of 3 inches.

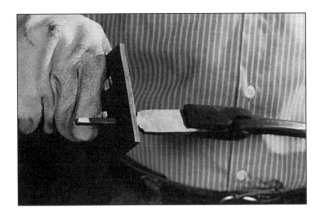

A ruler or caliper can be used to check the size of the tang as it is being drawn, but a better method is to use a heavy tool steel gauge with a $1/4$-inch square hole punched in it.

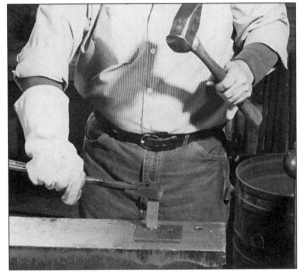

When the tang has been completed, place the gauge over the hardie hole, take another light yellow heat, grip the blank from the side, and drive the tang down through the gauge. This will help square up the tang and create clean, square shoulders for the tool's handle to rest against.

Now grip the completed tang in your tongs, heat the rest of the blank to a light yellow, and begin drawing out the blade. The object here is to draw a blade that flares evenly from shoulder to tip and tapers in width, from $1/4$-inch at the shoulder to approximately $1/16$-inch at the tip or bevel end. This will take a number of heats. Use heavy, rapid blows.

When the blade has been drawn to shape, take a lemon heat, place the end of the blade on the anvil's cutting table, and hammer a hot cut into the end at a 70° angle. Place a protractor set at 70° on the anvil face parallel to the tool's centerline to guide in getting the angle right.

Several blows may be required. Do not attempt to cut clear through the blade, this will cause the hot tip to fly off unpredictably. Instead, cut approximately two-thirds of the way through, then clamp the tip in the vise along the line of the cut, grip the blade at the shoulder (not the more delicate tang) with your tongs, and bend the blade back and forth until it breaks free.

Because the thickness of the blade tapers from shoulder to tip, this cutting edge is thinner at the point than it is at the heel. So reheat the end of the blade and forge the heel out, checking periodically to see that the edge is the same thickness from tip to heel. This will cause some distortion of the blade profile, but that will be corrected later during finishing. It will also change the skew angle from 70° to the desired 60°.

Now take another lemon heat and smooth the surfaces of the tool's shank by laying the tool on the anvil, placing a flatter atop it, and hammering the flatter along each surface.

The forging is now completed. Reheat the entire blade to just above its critical temperature. With this steel, the critical temperature is the point at which it no longer attracts a magnet. Then quickly bury the blade in a bucket of ashes to anneal it.

Pre-Heat Treatment Finishing

When the blade has completely cooled to room temperature, it's ready for pre-heat treatment finishing.

The first step is to grind the profile to the desired size and shape. This is the time to true up the side so that the tang projects perfectly along the tool's centerline, to true the tang if need be, and to make sure that the bevel end is at the desired angle.

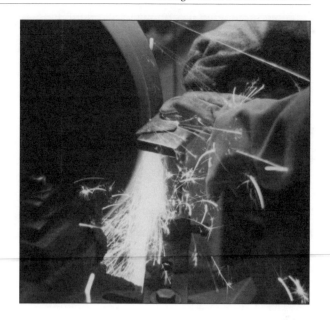

The next step is to create the double bevel. This can be done on a grinder, but a flat belt sander works even better because it produces the dead flat bevels you're looking for on this tool. Use a protractor or pre-set bevel gauge to verify your angle.

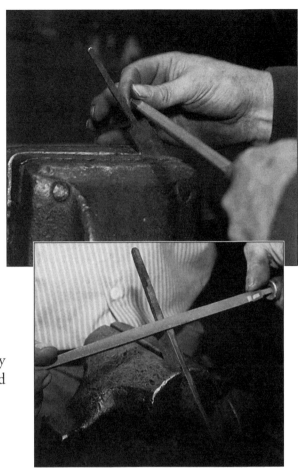

Now take the blade to the bench and finish it up by filing the shoulders square and even and dressing and deburring all over with coated abrasive.

TO POLISH OR NOT

I personally prefer to leave the shanks of my carving tools in a black or as-forged condition. Grinding, sanding, and polishing the shank of a tool doesn't improve its performance, which, after all, is the ultimate test of a tool.

Many woodworkers like a polished tool, however, and if this is what you want, now is the time do your preliminary polishing work. Start by hitting each surface briefly with 60-grit coated abrasive on a flat belt sander. This will reveal any high spots that need to be taken down on the grinder. Continue this back-and-forth regimen until the tool's surfaces are perfectly flat and bright.

This is as far as you can take your polishing before heat treatment. Hardening and tempering will discolor the tool, so final finishing will have to be done later.

HEAT TREATMENT

The skew chisel is now ready for heat treatment.

The first step is to <u>slowly</u> heat the bevel end of the tool to its critical temperature, removing it from the fire frequently and testing it with a magnet.

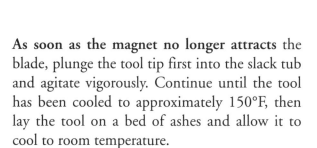

As soon as the magnet no longer attracts the blade, plunge the tool tip first into the slack tub and agitate vigorously. Continue until the tool has been cooled to approximately 150°F, then lay the tool on a bed of ashes and allow it to cool to room temperature.

To test the edge for hardness, run a smooth file over it. If the file skates over the surface, you've done a good job. If it bites in, you need to repeat the hardening process, checking the various parameters to see that you've carried out the operation correctly.

At this point, your skew chisel is too hard to use and needs to be tempered.

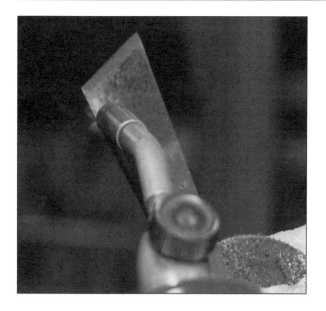

Start by polishing the bevels lightly on the sander or with a piece of coated abrasive in your hand so that the surfaces are clean and shiny. Then reheat the end of the blade <u>slowly</u> with a propane torch, watching for the desired tempering color, in this case straw to deep straw. When the color develops, immediatley plunge the tool into the slack tub again. Heat treatment is now completed.

Post-Heat Treatment Finishing

Now we need to finish up our chisel.

If you're polishing your tool all over, now is the time to complete this operation. Start by hitting all of the surfaces of the shank with 220-grit coated on the belt sander. Be very careful here. Even light sanding generates enough heat to spoil a tool's temper.

When all of the surfaces are clean and bright again, switch to progressively finer flap, Scotch-Brite, or Shur-Brite type polishing and blending wheels, which are available from most industrial supply houses. These products are capable of producing a mirror finish.

The next step is to sharpen the bevels. I like to start with a coarse diamond stone and continue on with progressively finer natural stones. You should do what works best for you.

When the bevels are done, it's time to handle the tool.

Because our version of the skew chisel has no bolster, we need to punch out a washer that slides up the tang, coming to rest at the blade's shoulder. This will act as a bolster.

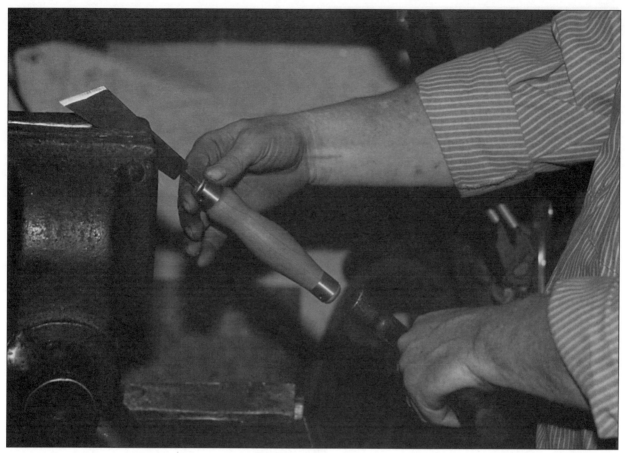

With the washer in place, grip the blade in a vise by the shank (not the heat-treated edge) and drive the handle onto the tang.

Our skew chisel is now finished.

9 MAKING A HOLLOWING ADZE

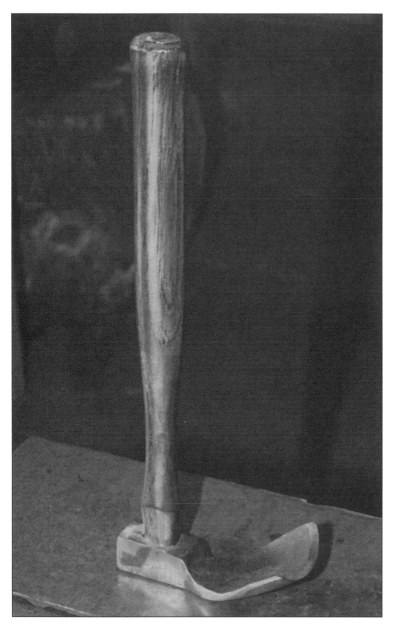

The hollowing adze is a more challenging tool to make. It involves a lot of heavy drawing, the drifting of an eye, and the forming of a curved and swept blade. It also calls for some layout work.

The hollowing adze is an extremely versatile tool.

Carvers use it for roughing out. Swung properly, it can remove large quantities of waste, quickly and with surprising accuracy. It is also indispensable for general hollowing work when making gutters, bowls, and chair seats.

The lightweight version we are making here has a 3-inch blade with a moderate bend and sweep and an inside bevel. This is a popular configuration but in practice, many combinations of bend, sweep, and bevel type (inside, outside, and double) are employed. You may want to experiment to find the configuration that suits you best.

Our adze is fitted with a 14-inch hickory handle and is designed to be used primarily with one hand.

LAYING OUT AND DRILLING

The blank for our hollowing adze is a piece of 1-inch square AISI 1080 high carbon steel 4-inches long.

Begin by laying out the tool on the blank. To do this, divide the blank in half lengthwise with a ruler and score this midpoint with a carbide-tipped scribe. This gives us a two-inch length of blank for the tool's eye section and another two-inch length for the blade.

Now cut a shallow (approximately $1/64$-inch deep) kerf along this scribed line with a hacksaw so the line will be readily visible when the blank is heated to forging temperature.

Divide the eye section in half lengthwise and score, then divide the eye section widthwise and score again. The cross formed by these two lines is the center of the eye section.

Lay a ruler along the lengthwise centerline of the eye section and score two more lines, each $3/16$ of an inch from — and on either side of — the center line widthwise. Mark these two intersections with a prick punch.

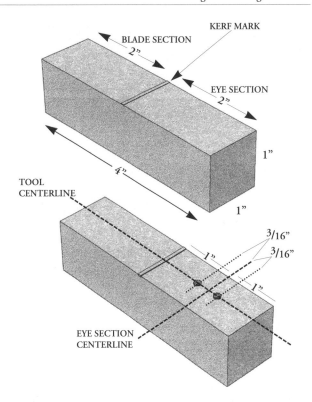

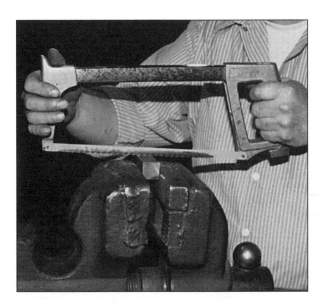

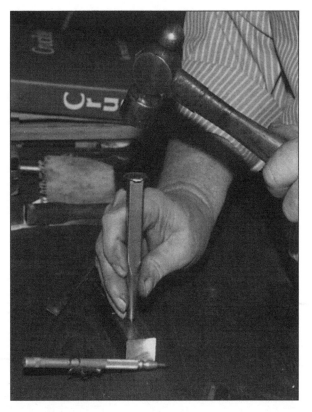

Now take the blank to the drill press and drill two 3/8-inch holes in the eye section, using the marks made by the prick punch as starting points. The result should be two 3/8-inch, side-by-side holes along to the tool's centerline in the middle of the eye section. These holes will be drifted out later during the forging sequence to form the tool's eye.

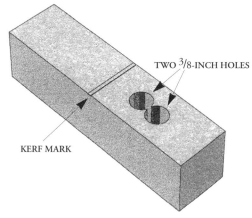

TWO 3/8-INCH HOLES

KERF MARK

Forging the Head

Grip the blank in an appropriately sized pair of tongs, place in the forge or furnace (a furnace is being used here), and heat all over to a light yellow. Be sure to soak the blank for 30 seconds or so to get a good, through heat.

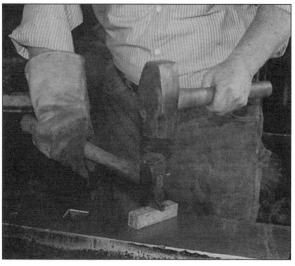

When the blank has reached the correct temperature, remove, place on the anvil and drive a fuller a half-inch deep into the kerfed centerline to divide the blade and eye sections. This takes some oomph so use the heaviest hammer you can swing. An eight-pound sledge is being used here. This operation could also be performed by hammering the workpiece onto a bottom fuller placed in the hardie hole or clamped in a leg vise.

DRAWING OUT THE BLADE

When the fullering is completed, grip the blank by the eye section, take another heat, position the blank so that the fuller impression is on the bottom and straddles the edge of the anvil, and begin drawing out the blade. This will take a number of heats.

When the blade is approximately ³/₈-inch thick, begin fullering to spread the blade to the desired width without over-lengthening it. Continue fullering and hammering out until the desired blade shape is achieved.

Then reheat the entire blade to just above its critical temperature and quickly bury it in a bucket of ashes to anneal it.

DRIFTING THE EYE

After the tool has cooled, grip the blade with an appropriately sized pair of tongs, insert the eye section in the forge or furnace, and take a lemon heat.

When it's ready, remove the tool, place the eye section over the hardie hole (or a punching plate if the hardie hole is oversized, as here), and hammer a tapered eye drift down into the two drilled holes. Use the heaviest hammer possible.

An eye-shaped cavity will begin to form. When the drift is approximately two-thirds of the way through, stop drifting and hammer the blank free of the drift.

Cool the drift in the slack tub. Reheat the tool, turn it over, and drift from the other side. Square up the sides of the eye section as the drifting proceeds. The result should be a perfectly shaped eye with an hour-glass cross section.

PRE-HEAT TREATMENT FINISHING

Grind the profile to the desired shape, then grind the cutting edge.

A 30-degree bevel works best. Thinner edges won't stand up to the battering these tools take. Thicker edges won't cut cleanly.

Take the time to grind a nice, crowned face on the poll, it makes a handy hammer. File and sand all rough edges.

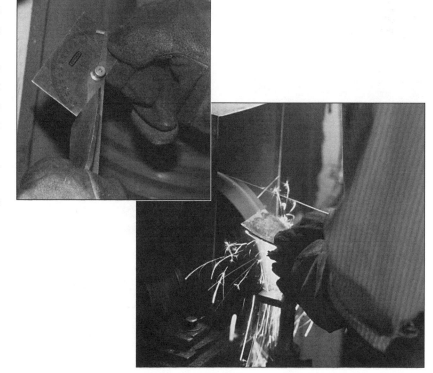

FORMING THE BLADE

The trick to forming the blade is to generate the bend and sweep at the same time.

Heat the blade slowly and thoroughly to a lemon yellow, place it over a swage with the desired sweep (a swage block is being used here), and hammer the blade into the swage depression with a one-inch, handled fuller. A rounded ball-peen hammer will also do.

At the same time, lift the tongs slowly, allowing the blade to bend from back to front as it sinks into the swage and bends from side to side.

When you've achieved the bend and curve you want, check the tool from on end to make sure the blade is perfectly perpendicular to the eye. Take out any wind or misalignment by reheating and adjusting the blade in the vise.

ADDITIONAL PRE-HEAT TREATMENT FINISHING

Clean up any rough spots by filing and sanding. It's especially important at this point to remove the decarburized layer of steel on the outside of the blade. A belt sander is ideal for this. Touch up the bevel as needed.

HEAT TREATMENT

Our hollowing adze is now ready for heat treatment.

The first step is to slowly heat the end of the blade to just above its critical temperature. When the correct temperature has been reached, plunge the tool straight down into a quench tank filled with light oil and agitate vigorously for at least 30 seconds.

Oil is used as the quenchant here because oil works more slowly than water. The tool's edge won't get as hard this way as it would with water, but it will have a great deal more toughness than a water-quenched edge and that is what we are looking for on this tool: An extremely tough edge with moderate hardness.

When the tool has cooled to around 150°F, remove it from the quench tank, place it on a bed of ashes, and allow it to cool to room temperature. Then polish the edge lightly on a sander and temper the tool to further increase its toughness. I like to temper my hollowing adzes to a bright peacock, but the temper you pick will be the one that works best for you.

Post-Heat Treatment Finishing

Now the tool needs to be handled. Begin by clamping the tool upside down in a vise and chamfering the bottom edge of the eye with a file. A die grinder, if you have one, will do this faster.

Place the tool upside down on the anvil and drive an appropriately sized handle into the eye with a heavy hammer. Note that the chamfer helps ease the handle into the eye by compressing the wood fibers as the handle is driven home.

When the handle is seated tightly, clamp the tool upright by its handle in a vise and apply a generous amount of wood swelling compound (Chair-Lok is being used here) to the handle's slot and protruding end. Drive a wooden wedge into the slot in as deeply as possible.

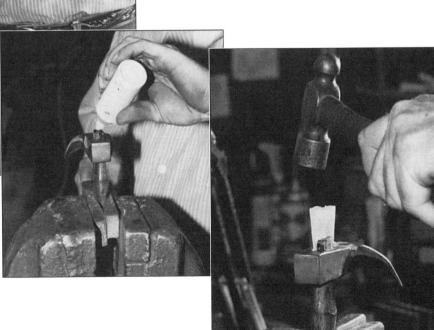

Trim off any excess, and finish by driving in a steel wedge angled 45 degrees to the wooden wedge.

After a good sharpening, our hollowing adze is ready to use.

MAKING YOUR OWN EYE DRIFTS

Eye drifts aren't available commercially but no matter, they're easy enough to make.

A 12-inch piece of 1¹/₂-inch round or square AISI 1060 to 1080 high carbon steel is a good blank for most any size eye drift. A 12-inch chunk of 1¹/₈ inch or 1¹/₄ inch pavement breaker tool will also do in a pinch.

To make an eye drift, mark off four inches and forge this portion of the blank as close as you can to the to the cross-section you want. This could be oval, round, square, or rectangular depending on the tool it is intended for.

Leave the remaining eight-inch portion as is. It will serve as a handle.

Anneal.

When the tool has cooled, grind the forged section so that it exactly matches the cross section of the handle you plan to use.

Now grind a ¹/₃₂-inch per inch taper down the working portion of the drift. This allows the tool to generate an eye with an hour-glass type cross section when used from both sides. It also helps prevent the drift from getting stuck in the workpiece.

Finally, grind a tapered point on the tip of the drift so it will penetrate the workpiece more easily.

Do not heat treat your drifts. And when cooling them during use, dip them in and out of the slack tub so that they are cooled rather than quenched. Repeated quenching, even when inadvertent, will embrittle your eye drifts and cause them to fail in service.

If your drift is to be used to create an eye with a traditional adze-type cross section, increase the taper to ¹/₁₆-inch per inch and use from one side only.

10 HOOK TOOL FOR WOODTURNING

Our turner's hook is made of oil-hardening tool steel. It's a good project for learning how to work this more challenging material.

Turner's hook tools are used to clean out the insides of hollow forms such as semi-enclosed vessels. They permit the turner to work areas that standard, straight-shanked tools can't reach. And because they slice rather than scrape, they give a good finish in a hard to finish area.

A wide variety of hook tools with different diameters and different reaches is required for this kind of work. There are no set rules for making these tools and turners will want to experiment with different diameters, different reaches, and different bevel combinations to find out what works best for them.

The hook we are making here has a small (approximately $1/2$-inch diameter) hook, a long (approximately $3^1/2$-inch) reach, and an inside bevel.

FORGING THE HOOK

The blank for our hook tool is a piece of $1/2$-inch round AISI 0-1 oil hardening bar $13^{1}/_{2}$-inches long.

Begin by heating three inches of the blank to forging temperature (a light yellow) in a forge or furnace. Remember to soak the blank thoroughly.

When the blank is ready, bring it to the anvil and forge a 5-inch long rectangular section $1/2$-inch wide and $1/8$-inch thick on the heated end. When the section is done, the forged end of the blank needs to be annealed.

To anneal, heat the forged end uniformly to a bright cherry, hold it at that temperature for two hours, cool it slowly in the fire to just under a medium cherry, then remove from the fire and set it aside to cool to room temperature.

PRE-HEAT TREATMENT FINISHING

When the blank has cooled, true up the profile of the forged section on the grinder.

Then grind a 1½-inch long, 30-degree bevel or cutting edge on the end of the tool. This is done now because our hook tool has an inside bevel and inside bevels are difficult to grind after the hook is formed.

FORMING THE HOOK

Reheat the tool. When the correct temperature has been reached, bring the tool to the horn of the anvil and bend the forged section or arm 45 degrees to the shank. This could also be done by bending the arm in a blacksmith's vise.

Straighten the arm on the anvil's face as necessary.

Clamp a bick in the vise, take another heat, lay the blade on the tip of the bick with the bevel on the inside and begin forging the hook. It may take several heats to get the hook just right. A 3/8-inch or 1/2-inch round bar clamped in the vice could also be used for this operation.

Anneal as detailed on page 131, and clean up the bevel with a file as needed.

Our hook tool is ready for heat treatment.

To harden the tool, heat the hook portion slowly and clear through to a cherry, then quench in oil, agitating rapidly until the temperature of the tool has been reduced to 150°. Then set aside on a bed of ashes to cool further to room temperature.

At Genuine Forgery we have found that many of these tools can be used in the as-hardened state, without tempering. Give it a try. If you experience edge crumbling during use, temper back until you get the toughness you require.

POST-HEAT TREATMENT FINISHING

Sharpen the hook by polishing the outside on a belt sander and touching up the inside with a die grinder or carver's slip.

It's a good idea to grind back the heel of the hook at this point to improve clearance. Go carefully here. Grind lightly and cool the tool frequently so that the temper isn't ruined.

To handle the turner's hook, drill a ³/8-inch hole 3¹/2-inches deep in the handle for the shank. Pour equal amounts of epoxy and hardener into the hole, mix thoroughly in the hole with a thin stick, and seat the shank. Let set overnight before using. It's important to epoxy the shank in the handle because of the amount of torque a hook tool develops in use. Without epoxy, the tool would quickly work itself loose.

Our woodturner's hook tool is now completed.

11 MAKING A MORTISING CHISEL

The mortising chisel must be forged exactly square, true, and to specified dimensions if it is to do its job well. This presents some interesting challenges to the beginning tool maker.

The mortising chisel is used to chop mortises. It comes in many sizes, from big, heavy, sometimes all-steel versions used to cut the large, deep mortises found in post and beam construction, to smaller ones used in cabinetmaking.

Mortising chisels take a beating. They're always driven with a hammer or mallet, and are required to wedge out heavy chips of often tough material. Because of this, they are extremely rugged in their construction.

The version we are making here has a ¹/₂-inch wide blade 7-inches long, and is fitted with a double-hooped, hardwood handle. This is a very versatile size mortising chisel capable of doing a wide range of work.

Forging the Chisel

The blank for our mortising chisel is a 6^{1}/$_{2}$-inch piece of ^{13}/$_{16}$-inch round AISI 1080 high carbon steel.

Grip the blank in an appropriately sized pair of tongs, place in the forge or furnace, and heat approximately 2 inches of the blank to a light yellow. Be sure to soak the blank for 30 seconds or so to get a good, through heat.

Now begin the tool by fullering off one inch of the blank for a tang (a spring fuller is being used here). Then begin drawing out the tang. Continue until you have a ^{3}/$_{8}$-inch square tang 3-inches long.

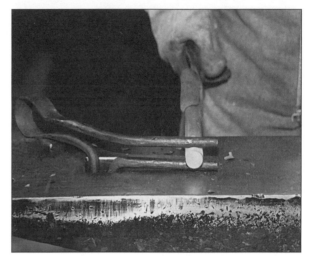

Jump the tool in a ³/8-inch square gauge to get a good, clean shoulder on the tool's shank.

Reverse the tool, grip with an appropriately sized pair of tongs, and begin roughing out the blade.

If a mortising chisel is to produce clean, tight joints, the sides of the chisel and the top and bottom of the chisel must be perfectly parallel and perpendicular to each other. To get sides that are perfectly parallel to each other and exactly ¹/₂ inch wide, set your vernier caliper to ⁹/₁₆ of an inch and forge the chisel to that size. This will produce a slightly oversized tool that can be ground later, during pre-heat treatment finishing, to exact size and parallelism. Also check the blade of the chisel frequently with a square to assure that the sides are as perpendicular to the top and bottom as possible. And check the top and bottom of the developing blade for straightness.

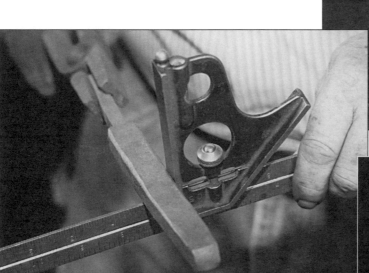

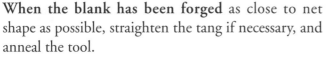

When the blank has been forged as close to net shape as possible, straighten the tang if necessary, and anneal the tool.

To anneal the tool, reheat the entire blade to just above its critical temperature. With the steel we're using here, that's the point when it no longer attracts a magnet. Then quickly bury the blade in a container of ashes and let it cool slowly to room temperature.

Pre-Heat Treatment Finishing

When the tool has cooled to room temperature, it's time to begin grinding it to the exact dimensions desired. Check frequently for parallelism and squareness as the grinding proceeds.

When the tool has been ground as close to final shape as possible, take it to the belt sander for final sizing and finishing.

When the shank is done, cut a 25 degree bevel on the sander. This is a good, standard bevel for mortising chisels.

Now take the tool the bench and finish it up. File the shoulder of the tool dead square, and clean up all rough edges with 60-grit coated abrasive.

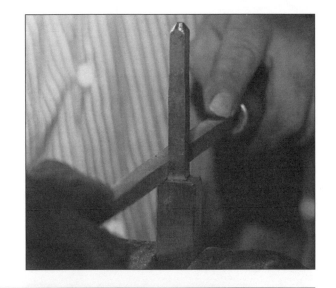

FINISHING

The mortising chisel is now ready for heat treatment. Begin by slowly heating the bevel end of the tool to its critical temperature, testing it periodically with a magnet until the right temperature has been achieved. When the magnet no longer attracts the chisel, plunge the tool tip first into the slack tub and agitate rapidly until the tool has cooled to 150°F.

Now the tool requires tempering. To temper the tool, polish the bevel lightly, then reheat the end of the blade slowly and evenly with a propane torch until the desired tempering color is reached. At Genuine Forgery, we temper mortising chisels to a peacock, but the color you temper your chisel to is up to you. When the desired color appears, quickly plunge the tool into the slack tub again.

When heat treatment is completed, fit the tool with a washer-type bolster and a double-hooped handle. After a good sharpening, the chisel is ready to use.

12 SOME DESIGN CONSIDERATIONS

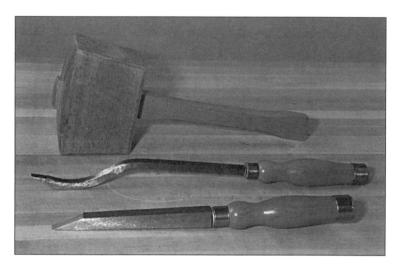

Forging is a fast, cost effective way to make high quality woodworking tools of virtually any size and shape. For woodworkers who use a lot of different tools, like carvers, it is a Godsend.

But making a tool is only half the story. How well a tool feels and works has as much to do with its design as it does its execution.

SOME DESIGN SUGGESTIONS

I've spent the last 25 years making woodworking tools. I've forged a lot of stuff during that time, from fancy, exotic tools made one at a time to production tools cranked out by the thousands. I've had a lot of success. And at least my share of failures.

One of the things I've learned along the way is that it isn't always easy to get started. You want to make a tool to solve a particular problem or do a specific job. But where do you start? And when you go to forge this tool, what will work and what won't?

These are questions I've asked myself many, many times over the years, and what follows are some of the answers I've come up with, as often as not by trial and error.

I'm including these suggestions as a way of helping you out of the starting blocks. They are not intended as the final word on tool making. Rather, they are jumping off points that will help you over some of the initial hurdles all beginning tool makers face, and get you making good tools faster.

I've been making the tools discussed in this section for more than 20 years. They're good tools and they continue to sell just as fast as I can make them. They have withstood the tests of time and close scrutiny. They will serve you well.

But as your confidence and abilities grow, don't be afraid to question the parameters set forth here or to try new things. Let your mind expand. Experiment. Innovate. In time you will come to see that a new bar of steel is like an empty canvas: Rife with interesting possibilities.

DRAWKNIVES

The drawknife is one of the oldest and most useful woodworking tools ever devised. It's been manufactured in hundreds of different configurations over the years, from giant ones used to shape ship masts in the age of sail to itty bitty ones still used in the making of fine baskets.

Drawknife blades should be tapered from back to front. A taper of from 1/4 inch at the back of the blade to 1/8 inch at the front on a standard sized blade is ideal. A tapered blade is superior to a flat blade. It's easier to grind a bevel on a tapered blade, and it's easier to sharpen one.

Tapering a drawknife blade at the anvil will cause it to curve or bow. Some woodworkers, like Windsor chair maker Mike Dunbar, leave this curve in. They feel it imparts a slicing action that helps the blade cut smoother and with less effort.

Keep the tangs on your drawknife on the same plane as the back of the blade. This gives the best control. A 25° bevel for the cutting edge works best, although some woodworkers prefer a 30° bevel.

INSHAVES

Inshaves are drawknives with curved blades. They are used for hollowing and rounding work.

Inshave tangs should be bent approximately 45° to the blade so the handles clear the workpiece. Tapering the ends of the handles will help maintain the necessary clearance.

Inshave blades can be shaped in an arc, circle, or rounded square or rectangle. Circular blades are by far the most popular for chair seat work. Inshave blades should be tapered just like drawknife blades. Grind a 25° bevel for a cutting edge.

COMBINATION DRAWKNIVES

The usefulness of drawknives can be greatly increased by forging a round depression or inshave shape into one end of the blade. This section can be used for both hollowing work, such as carving out chair seats, and shaving work, such as shaping tool handles.

If you plan to do a lot of handle work, leave the tang on the inshave end of the blade unbent or in line with the blade. This gives better working clearance.

SPOKESHAVES AND TRAVISHERS

Spokeshaves and travishers are miniature drawknives and inshaves. They are used to fine tune nearly completed workpieces. They can impart a fine finish on wood.

The blades are made the same way as drawknives except that the tangs are bent up at right angles to the blade. Taper these blades or forge a step in them so they're easier to sharpen. The blades should be about $^1/_{16}$ inch at the front. Grind with a 25° bevel.

ADZES

Adzes were utilized in every woodworking trade at one time but have fallen into disuse in this century. It's a shame, because the adze in its many forms is one of the most versatile and useful tools in the woodworker's arsenal.

THE UTILITY OR ALL-PURPOSE ADZE

An extremely versatile, all-purpose adze for dressing timbers and such can be forged from 1-inch-square tool making steel. The edge of the blade should be dished and have a bevel angle of around 30°.

This adze can be swung with one or two hands. If you intend to use it with one hand fit it with a 16- to 18-inch handle. If you intend to use both hands, use a 24- to 28-inch handle.

In some situations, you may find that you have to relieve the top of the cutting edge of this tool slightly.

This utility adze, a straight-bladed version of the traditional cooper's adze, can perform an extremely wide range of work.

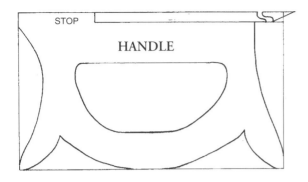

THE D-HANDLED OR HAND ADZE

This is one of the oldest forms of the wood-working adze. Its beauty lies in its simplicity: It requires no eye and thus is easily made of a light piece of steel.

A variety of straight, bent, and bent and swept shapes can easily be forged into the cutting end of these blades to do different kinds of carving and hollowing work. Lash or wire the blade securely to the top of a wooden, D-shaped handle and you're ready to go.

This heavy-duty hollowing adze, designed to be used with two hands, is ideally suited to all types of hollowing work.

HOLLOWING ADZES

Hollowing adzes are made in many sizes and shapes; the projects section of this book shows you how to make a nice, lightweight type.

A heavier, two-handed version suitable for hollowing out chair seats in a hurry can be made from a six inch piece of $1^{1}/_{4}$-inch square tool making steel. A bigger piece of steel will yield an even heavier, more powerful adze, but $1^{1}/_{4}$-inch square tool making steel is about as big a piece of steel a smith can forge without a helper.

This colt's foot adze with its radically curved blade can get into places other tools can't.

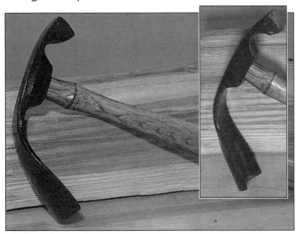

THE COLT'S FOOT ADZE

This radically shaped hollowing adze, known as a colt's foot adze because it is said to resemble the foot of a colt, is extremely useful for deep and unusual hollowing tasks.

Fit with a handle that suits you. Some woodworkers use an extremely short handle that can't interfere with the workpiece.

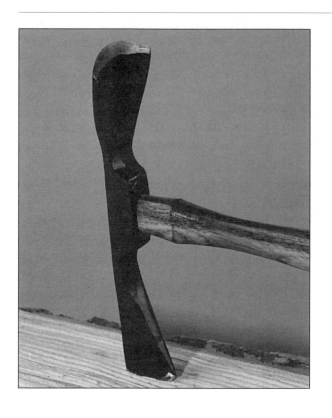

THE CARVER'S AND SCULPTOR'S ADZE

Carvers and sculptors use this tool for roughing out. It can be made in many variations, but the simple configuration of a hatchet-type blade on one end and a wide, fairly shallow, gouge-type blade on the other, has proved extremely popular over the years. I have made and sold more than 8,000 of these tools in the last 20 years.

Axes

The axe is the most basic of woodworking tools; its form was pretty much established in the Bronze Age.

Making a full-sized axe is a difficult undertaking for the beginning tool maker, but a handy, lightweight model suitable for working on carvings and such can easily be forged from a 4-inch piece of 1-inch square AISI 1078 high carbon steel.

Reserve 2 inches for an eye section and 2 inches for the blade. Fuller heavily to get a blade 3$\frac{1}{2}$ inches wide.

A lightweight side axe of the same design can be made by fullering and drawing the blade from one side only.

CHISELS AND GOUGES

Chisels and gouges are used in every branch of woodworking. They are all made following the basic precepts outlined in the projects section of this book.

THE SWAN NECK CHISEL

A 12-inch piece of $3/8$-inch square high carbon or water hardening tool steel makes a good blank for a cabinetmaker's swan neck chisel. For a heavier tool suitable for post and beam work, start with a 15-inch blank of $1/2$-inch square tool making steel.

SLICKS AND PATTERN MAKER'S CHISELS

Generally speaking, chisels should be made so that the cutting edge, shank, tang, and handle are perfectly in line. This assures that the full force of the user's thrust is applied to the cutting edge and that the tool cuts true.

Pattern maker's chisels, used to do paring work below the surface of a workpiece, and slicks, used to dress long workpieces, are exceptions to this rule. These chisels need offset or cranked shanks to allow the user's hand to clear the workpiece.

For improved control, a second, knob-like handle can be bolted to the blade of the slick to enable it to be used like a plane.

The off-set shank and handle of this three-inch slick allows it to be used like a plane on long paring jobs.

PNEUMATIC CHISELS

Many serious carvers use special chisels mounted in pneumatic hammers to speed their work.

It's easy to make any size or type chisel for these hammers, but you have to have a factory-made tool to start with. That's so you can replicate the shank. Different hammers employ different shanks and they're not interchangeable. Keep these tools simple and beefy.

CARVER'S GOUGES

In his landmark book, <u>The Making of Tools</u> (see appendix), Alexander Weygers sets forth an interesting and innovative design for carver's gouges. His theory makes a lot of sense and you might want to give it a try.

What Weygers says, basically, is that in order to track well and cut cleanly, a carving gouge should have a cone-shaped blade with a cutting edge that slants forward. When configured this way, he says, the upper edges of the blade enter the workpiece first, severing the outer grain of the wood and assuring that the chip or waste trapped in the tool is quickly and easily freed without binding.

North Carolina woodworker Drew Langsner has taken Weygers' idea one step further and has applied his theory to a heavy duty, chair seat hollowing adze. After considerable testing, Langsner reports that the tool cuts easier and cleaner than traditional hollowing adzes.

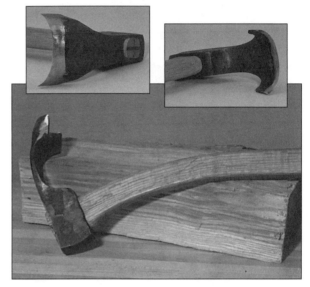

This heavy-duty chair seat adze was designed by Drew Langsner and utilizes Alexander Weyger's gouge shape theory for improved cutting.

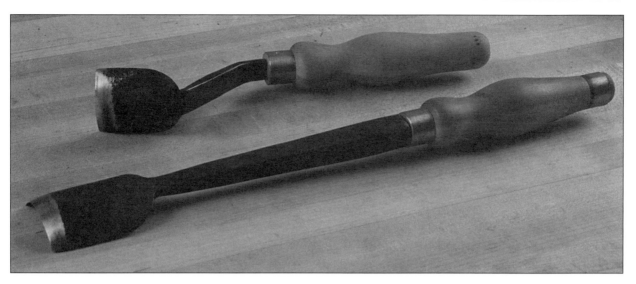

The hollowing shave, top, and the saddling gouge have proved extremely useful for a wide range of carving and finishing chores.

THE SADDLING GOUGE

This tool was originally designed to do the saddling work required when building certain types of log cabins. But it proved so effective that chair makers and carvers are now buying it as well.

The tool is made from a 7-inch piece of $^{13}/_{16}$-inch round tool making steel. An interesting element to the tool is the design of the shank. By leaving the blank at full diameter where the shank meets the tang, a strong, natural shoulder is formed. This shoulder serves as a heavy duty bolster that will stand up to years of hard use.

HOLLOWING SHAVES

Hollowing shaves are small, double-cranked gouges used to clean out bowls, chair seats, and such. The double-cranked shank allows the woodworker to get into places that can't be reached with normal tools. Adjust the angles to suit the job.

MEASURING TOOLS

It's easy to make a lot of your own measuring tools. AISI 1095 carbon steel is an excellent material for items like bevel gauges, calipers, and go/no go gauges for specific applications.

Floor anneal these tools after forging. This gives them just the right temper.

THE COMPASS/SCRIBE

In his extraordinary book, <u>Blacksmith's Manual Illustrated</u> (see appendix), J.W. Lillico offers a host of interesting and provocative ideas about complex, integral or one-piece forgings.

The compass/scribe is a good example of this. At first glance, the tool looks complicated and hard to make. But a closer examination shows that the frame is really just one forging made from a single 16-inch piece of $1/2$-inch by $3/16$-inch AISI 1095 high carbon steel.

Complicated-looking tools can easily be made from a single piece of steel if you think about it and are open to experimenting

FROES

Froes are used to split or rive wood. They were found everywhere at one time and were used to split out boards and shingles. They're not seen around as much anymore, but many woodturners still rely on them to prepare stock for the lathe.

The tool consists of a long blade with an eye on one end. In practice the blade is driven into the workpiece with a club or mallet while the handle fitted to the eye is worked back and forth, helping the wood to split apart.

The eyes of froes were traditionally welded

A woodturner's double caliper, top, and a machinist's caliper, both forged from AISI 1095 and floor annealed for many years of rugged service.

The frame of this compass/scribe, staring with the pencil holder at one end and ending with the pivot leg on the other, is forged from a single piece of high-carbon steel.

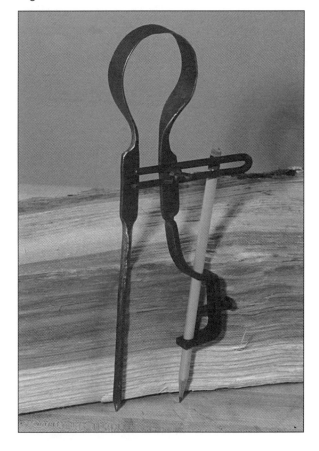

up in the forge, but an even stronger one can be made by drifting one out of a 1¹⁄₄-inch square or larger piece of steel. Draw down the rest of the steel to form your blade.

A DOUBLE-HANDLED FROE

The double-handled froe illustrates another piece of innovative thinking.

Instead of trying to bolt or weld a second handle onto the froe's blade, simply slit one end of the blade into two tangs with a hot cut or abrasive saw. Leave one tang in line with the blade and bend the other 90° so that it can be used to work the tool back and forth.

A lot of old hay knives utilize this idea.

This double-handed froe offers an interesting solution to a design problem.

PLANE IRONS

The beginning blacksmith can easily make any size or type plane iron.

Always taper blades intended for use in old wooden planes, the taper keeps them locked tightly at the desired setting.

For single-iron planes, use stock as thick as the mouth will bear to keep chatter and vibration to a minimum.

Cap irons for double-iron planes are easily made. Drill the hole for the cap iron screw head with the appropriately sized drill, lay out the screw slot, drill the appropriately sized hole at the bottom of the slot, and saw the slot out with a hacksaw. Dress with files as needed.

REAMERS

Woodworkers use a lot of reamers, from simple types uses to ream out handles for tangs, to fancy sets used to make and sound bagpipes.

Half-round and hollow reamers are hard to make, but most reaming jobs can be done with a flat reamer. Relieve the edges so they will cut better and the tool won't bind in the hole.

Take some time to true your reamer so that it runs straight without a lot of wobbling. Forge a tapered square tang on the end of the shank if you intend to use it in a brace. A simple round tang works in a hand drill or drill press.

WEDGES

Wedges are used to split out workpieces from logs. In order for a wedge to work well, it should be approximately 12-inches long and should taper from 1-inch at the head to less than 1/16-inch at the bit. Floor anneal for just the right toughness.

HAMMERS

Blacksmiths can make every type hammer used in woodworking. I like square faces on my hammers because they can reach into corners.

The big, square-faced claw hammer at the back of this photo weighs five pounds and is intended for heavy-duty wrecking and erecting jobs. It is shown here with a standard hammer to illustrate its relative size.

Here a holdfast is used to secure a carver's adze to the workbench so the adze can be worked on hands free.

WORK HOLDING DEVICES

Good work holding devices can easily be made at the anvil.

For timber work, forge up a pair of log dogs to pin your workpiece solidly in place. The chisel ends of these tools should be at right angles to each other and well tapered. This makes it easier to drive them into the workpiece and the support logs beneath it.

For bench work, forge up a few holdfasts that can be used to clamp smaller workpieces in place.

A 12-inch piece of 9/16-inch AISI 1080 is a good blank for these. Floor anneal them for just the right amount of spring. Use with a 5/8-inch hole.

GOOD DESIGN

What makes for good design?

For this I advise you to study woodworking tools made between 1820 and 1920 — especially the Cast Steel tools manufactured in Sheffield, England — when the ability to make and use hand tools was highly developed and top-notch materials were readily available. See how tools were designed and made to enable carpenters, cabinetmakers, and the like to do good, fast work, day in and day out, year after year.

Studying old tools will also show you the great diversity of approaches that were taken in the old days to accomplish a given task. This is one aspect of tool technology that never ceases to amaze me: The number of diverse solutions to a particular problem.

An interesting example of this can be found in Henry C. Mercer's <u>Ancient Carpenters' Tools</u>. A lifelong collector of early American woodworking tools, Mercer notes that many early tools were made in a wide variety of configurations. He points out, for example, that cooper's adzes, which were also used to hollow out bowls, canoes, bee hives and the like, came with single bevels on top, single bevels on the bottom, and all manner of double bevels in between.

Another example is the wide range of ship builder's caulking irons manufactured in this country in the 19th and early 20th centuries. When asked why there were so many sizes and shapes, one maker replied: "It is largely due to the whims and fancies of the men who use them. At our company, we have catered to these fancies, contending that is it none of our business <u>what</u> a man wanted, it was our business to <u>make</u> whatever he wanted, as he wanted it...."

Yet another example is the extremely wide range of bill hooks found in early English pattern books. As R.A. Salaman notes in his monumental <u>Dictionary of Tools</u>: "Tool makers of the 19th and early 20th Centuries... listed up to a hundred types of Bill Hooks, and even today the makers can supply a wide range. Whether differences in shape in general reflect any significant difference of function is doubtful... It seems more probable that this remarkable variety in type was designed to meet a persistent local demand. Before the factories took over, farm workers and householders bought from a local tool-smith whose business was later captured by the factory only if the customer could still be supplied with the particular shape to which he and his forebears had become accustomed."

From the old days it is clear that there is no single best way to do something; what is best, it turns out, is what works best for you.

This is a very liberating idea. When you know how to make your own tools, you aren't bound by what someone else thinks is good. You are free, instead, to experiment, and to discover what is good for you.

Now, get it lit and get it hit.

This engraving of Sheffield style tools showing axes and adzes, was reprinted from <u>The Cutting Edge: An Exhibition of Sheffield Tools.</u>

APPENDIX

SOURCES FOR STEEL, BLACKSMITHING EQUIPMENT, AND SHOP SUPPLIES

ALBRACO Metals Corp., 219 Westbury Ave., Carle Place, L.I., NY 11514. Ph: (800) ALBRACO (252-7226). Fax: (516) 334-1933.
Sells a wide variety of tool steels in most shapes and sizes.

Amory Forge, Ph: (519) 855-4986.
U.S. distributor for Kohlswa cast steel anvils made in Sweden.

ARBEE Sales Co., 313 North Morgan St., Chicago, IL 60607-1381. Ph: (312) 829-1468. Fax: (312) 829-9561.
The No. 1 supplier of reasonably priced hydraulic equipment and supplies. Catalogue contains excellent information on designing and building your own hydraulic systems.

Burden's Surplus Center, P.O. Box 82209, Lincoln, NE 68501-2209. Ph: (800) 228-3407.
Offers a wacky assortment of industrial equipment at reasonable — and sometimes bargain — prices.

Cardinal Engineering, Inc., RR 1, Box 163-1, Cameron, IL 61423.
Sells tool making steels and related supplies. Catalogue available for $2.

Centaur Forge Ltd., 117 North Spring St., P.O. Box 340, Burlington, WI 53105-0340. Ph: (414) 763-9175. Fax: (414) 763-8350.
The most comprehensive supplier of blacksmithing equipment in the country. Everything is new, and consequently somewhat pricey.

Cutter Northern Refractories, 49 Atheletic Field Rd., Waltham, MA 02154. Ph: (617) 894-7916.
Sells refractories and furnace parts; also designs and builds forging furnaces.

Enco Manufacturing Co., Ph: (800) 860-3400. Fax: (800) 860-3500. Enco has branches throughout the country. These are the numbers for their main office in Chicago.
A good, price-competitive purveyor of industrial supplies, most of it made offshore.

Furnaces, Ovens, & Baths, Inc., 4906 White Lake Rd., Clarkston, MI 48346-2639. Ph: (810) 625-7400. Fax: (810) 625-4030.
A well known supplier of used forging furnaces. Also sells miscellaneous furnace parts.

Glendale Forge, Monk Street, Thaxted, Essex CM6 2NR, England. Ph: 011-44-1371-830466. Fax: 011-44-1371-831419.
Manufactures and sells a wide range of blacksmithing tools. A catalogue and price list are available for $5.

W.W. Grainger, Inc.
Grainger has hundreds of branch offices. Check your phone book for the branch that serves your area. One of the largest suppliers of shop equipment in the world. An excellent source for hard-to-find motors. Prices are on the high side.

Harbor Freight Tools, 3491 Mission Oaks Blvd., P.O. Box 6010, Camarillo, CA 93011-6010. Ph: (800) 423-2567. Fax: (805) 445-4900.
Very large supplier of low-priced equipment made offshore. Pick carefully. Some of it's good, some of it isn't. Catalogue available for $2.

Hi-Heat Co., Inc., 32 Glendale Rd., South Windsor, CT 06074. Ph: (203) 528-9315. Fax: (203) 528-0421.
Supplies new and used furnaces — including forging furnaces.

Industrial Metal Supply Co., 7595 Raytheon Rd., San Diego, CA 92111. Ph: (819) 277-8200. Fax: (619) 277-3865.
Sells tool making steels.

Iron Age Antiques, Ocean View, DE 19970. Ph: (302) 539-5344 or (302) 539-6274.
An excellent source for used blacksmithing equipment of all kinds. Be warned, prices are high. Also offers rare and out-of-print books on blacksmithing and metalworking.

Jantz Supply, P.O. Box 584, Davis OK 73030. Ph: (405) 369-2316. Fax: (405) 369-3082.
Well-known supplier of knife-making kits and equipment, including a lot of gear useful in tool making.

Jere Kirkpatrick's Valley Forge & Welding, 30-C E. San Francisco St.,Willits, CA 95490. Ph: (707) 459-2523.
Makes and sells blacksmithing equipment, offers plans and a kit for a low-cost, foot-powered treadle hammer.

Koval Knives, 5819 Zarley St., P.O. Box 492, New Albany, OH 43054. Ph: (614) 855-0777.
Another big supplier of knife-making equipment.

McMaster-Carr Supply Co., P.O. Box 440, New Brunswick, NJ 08903-0440. Ph: (908) 329-3200. Fax: (908) 329-3772.
Competes with Grainger as an all-purpose supplier of virtually everything industrial. Pricey.

MSC Industrial Supply Co., 151 Sunnyside Blvd., Plainview, NY 11803-9915. Ph: (800) 645-7270 Fax: (800) 255-5067.
A good, comprehensive supplier of industrial goods of all kinds, including tool making steels. Prices are on the expensive side.

NC Tool Co., Inc., 6568 Hunt Road, Pleasant Garden, NC 27313. Ph: (800) 446-6498.
Makes high-quality standard and custom gas forges and related equipment.

Nolan Supply Corp., 111-115 Leo Ave., P.O. Box 6289, Syracuse, NY 13217. Ph: (800) 736-2204. Fax: (800) 463-2443.
Supplies tool making steels in any quantity. Also sells industrial supplies.

Northern Hydraulics, Inc., P.O. Box 1499, Burnsville, MN 55337. Ph: (800) 533-5545. Fax: (612) 894-0083.
Offers an eclectic assortment of equipment and supplies at reasonable prices. Very slow on delivery.

O.P. Link Handle Co., Inc., Salem, IN 47167. Ph: (812) 883-2981.
The nation's top supplier of tool handles.

Timbercove Trading Co., 121 H St., Petaluma, CA 94920. Ph: (707) 778-8261. Fax: (707)-778-0524.
U.S. distributor for Peddinghaus blacksmithing tools and equipment. Free price list on request.

Travers Tool Co., Inc., 128-15 256th Ave., P.O. Box 541550, Flushing, NY 11354-0108. Ph: 1-800-221-0270. Fax: 1-800-722-0703.
Offers high-quality but expensive industrial supplies and a very good selection of tool making steels.

Welders Warehouse, Inc., 20 Cortland St., Homer, NY 13077. Ph: (800) 777-6167. Fax: (607) 749-2961.
Offers a reasonably priced line of welding and shop supplies. Free catalog.

Wholesale Tool, Ph: (800)-521-3420. Wholesale Tool has branches throughout the country. This is the number for corporate headquarters in Warren, MI.
Another good, price-competitive source for a wide range of industrial supplies, including some tool making steels.

ORGANIZATIONS AND PERIODICALS OF INTEREST

Artist-Blacksmiths' Association of North America (ABANA), P.O. Box 206, Washington, MO 63090. Ph/Fax: (314) 390-2133.
Every woodworker contemplating making his or her own tools should join ABANA. It is a wellspring of knowledge and assistance on every aspect of blacksmithing, with affiliated chapters throughout the country. Membership includes a subscription to The Anvil's Ring, the ABANA quarterly, which is chock full of tips and other helpful information. The association also offers special deals to members on books and plans of interest to blacksmiths.

"Anvil" Magazine, "Voice of the American Farrier and Blacksmith", P.O. Box 1810, Georgetown, CA 95634 (916)-333-2142.
Published monthly.

"Blacksmith's Journal", Rt.1, Box 189, Lonedell, MO 63060 (314)-629-4061.
Published monthly. Call or write for a free sample issue.

"The Fine Tool Journal", 27 Fickett Rd. Pownal, ME 04069. Ph: (207) 688-4962.
Published quarterly.

HELPFUL BOOKS ON BLACKSMITHING AND TOOL MAKING

The following books are available from Norm Larson Books, 5426 E. Hwy. 246, Lompoc, CA 93436 Ph: (805)-735-2095. Many are also available from Centaur Forge and other dealers specializing in arts and crafts books.

The Art of Blacksmithing by Alex W. Bealer (Funk & Wagnalls Publishing Co., Inc., New York).
The "Bible" of the blacksmithing renaissance in America. A good, broad reference work.

Blacksmith's Manual Illustrated by J.W. Lillico (The Technical Press Ltd., London).
An advanced course in blacksmithing with emphasis on complex, integral forgings.

Blacksmithing for the Home Craftsman by Joe Pehoski (Stuhr Museum, Grand Island, NB).
Plainly written and packed with sound advice. The section on troubleshooting is especially helpful.

Blacksmiths' and Farriers' Tools at Shelburne Museum by H.R. Bradley Smith (Shelburne Museum, Inc., Shelburne, VT).
One of the best books available on blacksmithing tools.

Country Blacksmithing by Charles McRaven (Harper-Row, New York).
Great information on setting up from scratch. Guerrilla blacksmithing at its best.

Decorative and Sculptural Ironwork by Dona Z. Meilach (Crown Publishers, Inc., New York).
A thorough and interesting survey of contemporary blacksmithing featuring some of the country's finest practitioners.

New Edge of the Anvil by Jack Andrews (SkipJack Press, Inc., Ocean City, MD).
Another excellent book on setting up shop and getting going.

The Engineer's Guide to Steel by Albert Hanson and J. Gordon Parr (Addison-Wesley Publishing Co., Inc., Reading, MA).
A good, basic course on the manufacture and use of steel of all types.

Fine Woodworking on Hand Tools selected by the editors of "Fine Woodworking" magazine (The Taunton Press, Newtown, CT).
Practical information on tool making from the woodworker's perspective.

The Hand Forged Knife by Karl Schroen (Knife World Publications, Knoxville, TN).
American knife makers have led the charge in working modern tool steels in the craft shop. Schroen is among the most knowledgeable in this area.

Hardening and Tempering Engineer's Tools by George Gentry (Argus Book Ltd., Watford, England).
A well-written, easily understood treatise on the basics of heat treating.

Machinery's Handbook, A Reference Book for the Mechanical Engineer, Draftsman, Toolmaker and Machinist, edited by Holbrook L. Horton (Industrial Press, Inc., New York).
A comprehensive and indispensable reference book on modern metalworking. The latest edition is expensive so consider buying a two- or three-year old edition secondhand for smaller bucks.

The Making of Tools, The Modern Blacksmith, and The Recycling, Use and Repair of Tools, all by Alexander G. Weygers (Van Nostrand Reinhold Co., New York).
The "Holy Trinity" of guerrilla tool making. I'm still using many of the tricks I gleaned from Weygers years ago.

Practical Blacksmithing compiled and edited by M.T. Richardson, editor of "The Blacksmith & Wheelwright" (material originally published between 1889 and 1891 and reprinted by Weathervane Books, New York).
Thousands of words of sound advice from the real thing.

Tool Steel Simplified by Frank R. Palmer, George V. Luerssen, and Joseph S. Pendleton, Jr. (Chilton Co., Radnor, PA).
The best book available on tool steels and their uses.

WOODCARVING Tools, Materials, & Equipment by Chris Pye, (Guild of Master Craftsman Publications Ltd., East Sussex, England).
This book is a must for woodcarvers. The commentary on tool sharpening is particularly valuable.

The Work Methods and Tools of the Artist-Blacksmith by Otto Schmirler (Wasmuth Publishing, Tubingen, Austria).
An excellent, well-illustrated manual on making and using blacksmithing tools.

INTERESTING AND USEFUL BOOKS ON WOODWORKING TOOLS

Ancient Carpenter's Tools by Henry C. Mercer (published for the Bucks County Historical Society by Horizon Press).
An American "Goodman" (see below) containing a wealth of information.

The Antique Tool Collector's Guide to Value by Ronald S. Barlow (Windmill Publishing Co., El Cajon, CA).
The emphasis is on the dollar value of old tools but the illustrations are excellent, clear, and plentiful.

Country Craft Tools by Percy W. Blandford (David & Charles, London).
Offers rare insight into use of rural trade tools. The sections on heat treating and sharpening are very good.

Dictionary of American Hand Tools compiled by Alvin Sellens (published by the author, Augusta, KS).
A wonderful cornucopia of tool illustrations. Check out the Swinging Monkey on Page 467.

Dictionary of Tools by R.A. Salaman (George Allen & Unwin Ltd., London).
If you can afford to buy only one book on woodworking tools, this is it.

The History of Woodworking Tools by W.L. Goodman (David McKay & Co., Inc., New York).
A solid history of woodworking tools from ancient times to the present.

With Hammer in Hand by Charles F. Hummel (published for the Henry Francis du Pont Winterthur Museum by the University Press of Virginia, Charlottesville).
This detailed documentation of the famed Dominy workshops of East Hampton, NY, is a classic in woodworking tool history.

Woodworking Tools at Shelburne Museum by Frank H. Wildung (Shelburne Museum, Inc., Shelburne, VT).
A handy survey of early American woodworking tools and implements.

INDEX

Edited and photographed by
John Kelsey

Design and layout by
Morgan Kelsey

Index by
Harriet Hodges

Printed and bound at
Vaughan Printing
Nashville, TN